THE ACTIVE KILLER FALLACY

A TACTICAL TRAINING PRIMER FOR POLICE OFFICERS

by

Robin Kipling

Contents

Preface

1. *Simplicity, Flexibility, and Reality*
2. *Principles*
3. *Communication*
4. *Training Humans*
5. *Basic Formation*
6. *Training the Brain*
7. *Active Killing*
8. *Pushing Forward*

Acknowledgments and Sources

PREFACE

This book is a tactical training primer for uniformed and tactical operations police officers, military members, and their trainers, which focuses on internal team formation and movement.

Since 1998, I have been a police officer and have served in the highest crime areas of a busy major city as a street-level patrol officer, supervisor, tactical operator, and trainer of tactical operators. I have delivered training and developed curriculum in defensive tactics and officer safety–related subject matter throughout my career and have been declared by the courts as an expert in that field. This text encapsulates what I believe is the optimal approach to training.

In this primer, I will introduce a basic system of formation movement and communication in common use. From this starting point, I will introduce principles and rules of thumb that can be integrated to create a single flexible formation capable of working effectively in the highest number of situations.

This is not intended to be a comprehensive manual on building searches and entry. Containment, breaching, and external team movement are not discussed. This training primer seeks to apply truths and principles in a new way that will greatly enhance the effectiveness of your existing training in internal team movement. Furthermore, the truths and principles discussed in this primer can also be applied to enhance and improve all of your training programs in defensive tactics, tactical training, and beyond.

1

Simplicity, Flexibility, and Reality

*An inflexible army does not triumph,
An unbending tree breaks in the wind.
Thus, the rigid and inflexible will surely fail, While the soft and flowing will prevail.*
            Lao Tzu, Tao Te Ching

Team formation movement is a critical, force-multiplying tactic for police officers, peace officers, and protectors of all kinds; optimizing its effectiveness is an integral part of every officer's training.

The best formation for officers is the simplest formation. If we were to visualize the ideal tactical formation, it would look something like an amoeba: a moving organism with the capability of altering its shape and adapting to an ever-changing environment; a single, flexible formation as opposed to a different formation for each new environment or challenge.

Currently, the law enforcement community's approach to solving new tactical dilemmas—such as how to respond to a rapid mass murder like a school shooting—is deviating from practices already in place and adopting something new. This causes a breakdown in training. Police officers do not need a new tactical formation for every new challenge we face. Instead, we need to continue to do exactly what we already know how to do, but do it better. We need consistency and simplicity, not only within individual systems but also across different units of our law enforcement organizations.

Police organizations have specialty units that operate and communicate differently than front-line officers. When these different groups need to work together, the result is confusion. To avoid this, every unit in the organization needs to operate as consistently as possible at a basic level.

The greater the consistency in our training, the higher the probability of success. When we develop a new formation, such as a diamond formation, a three or five person tethered formation (three members walking forward, two walking backward), a Vee or Tee formation, they may look ideal on the chalkboard for a specific purpose, but its success in the field is unlikely, given the training realities that I will describe. When a new challenge emerges, such as the mass murder threats of the past 20 years, we invent something new to address it, then market that solution regardless of any evidence in the field that it works. New systems are appealing, like a new toy, and expertly marketed, but this approach to problem-solving is flawed and destined to fail. In this book, I'll explain why.

As police officers, we need a single type of formation, and it needs to be flexible. To achieve this, we must accomplish several goals. We must

- internalize core operating and personal training principles;
- follow a simple and reliable means of communication;
- obey a few rules of thumb; and
- remember the physiological factors of stress that will affect our performance.

As police trainers, we must accept the unfortunate reality that we don't have enough time or money to train officers competently for every possible situation. Instead, we must adjust our instruction to focus on the situations that our officers are most likely to encounter.

Operating Principles

We must embrace the basics and develop an intuitive understanding of the principles we all know, even though we are still tempted by the lure of a shiny new solution. Adaptations need to be made, yes, but the more we deviate from our basic operating practices, the closer to failure we move. When new challenges arise, that is precisely the time to return to the security of science and trusted principles rather than abandoning them.

Concepts such as John Boyd's **OODA Loop** or Charles Remsberg's **Thought Process** are two such reliable principles that offer an invaluable way of evaluating our formation tactics for effectiveness. To promote a deeper understanding of how these principles work, I've dedicated the next chapter to discussing them in depth. This understanding will be critical for moving forward in this book and in training, because exploring tactics is like opening Pandora's box. When "what if" discussions surface on training day, we need a tool to quickly determine which tactics are sound versus which ones are unsound, and then move on rather than squandering valuable training time. The OODA Loop and the Thought Process are tools that will help officers in the field and trainers in the classroom alike in evaluating tactics quickly and effectively.

Communication

Another component necessary for an effective and flexible formation is a dependable system of communication. Effective communication connects members of a team and gives them greater range and flexibility. Questions about what type of communication and language to use should yield to focusing on what is simple and usable for *the street-level officer with limited training*. This is a very important caveat. The aim of this primer is not to create perfect solutions but to suggest sound solutions that can be taught and retained in the amount of time available for training officers.

Furthermore, when the style of communication conforms to that used in the rest of your training program, you will improve not only your formation system but the entire curriculum by way of consistency. When communication and operating principles are consistent among all the members of an organization, from entry-level recruits to specialty units, the entire service is strengthened. When different police agencies are consistent with each other in their operating principles, tactics, and forms of communication, their work across an entire region or country is strengthened.

Communication is particularly important in formation training because it maintains the integrity of the formation so that it remains unified and true to its purpose; an adhesion that connects all its members yet allows each one of them to think and operate independently. Communication accomplishes this bond, and it can be achieved through verbal or nonverbal means. By using practices known as **reading off** and **squeezing up**, formation members add a nonverbal dimension to their communication that will enable them to maintain a constant visual and physical reference to each other. Another vital role of reading off is allowing for correction. Mistakes happen, and self-correcting measures need to built into the system to keep it functioning. I'll introduce such a system of communication in chapter 3.

Rules of Thumb and Physiology

Rules of thumb need to be layered into an effective system of tactical formation, and the **Tactical Thinking Model** helps us rank our priorities. **Bringing the "bad guys" to us**, as opposed to us going into the kill zone, and **dealing with the real threat versus the perceived threat** are some of the rules of thumb that will be presented throughout this book.

Another layer to consider is how officers experience the physiological effects of stress and fear. After all, we're training humans, not programming computers. Stress and fear cause physiological responses, such as an elevated heart rate, that have profound and well known effects on performance. For this reason, any tactical training primer would be remiss without a brief overview of the physiological effects of stress.

These physiological effects also need to be recognized and built-in when constructing a formation system. This recognition should lead to realistic expectations of what skills officers will be able perform in the field under duress. In chapter 4, I will discuss these effects in the context of this single formation theory and introduce some coping strategies that will help maximize performance.

As progressive trainers, we also need to acknowledge the research of experts outside of our field and apply that expertise to our own skills. For example, experts in the fields of sports physiology and psychology have made considerable advances in areas we haven't yet mastered. This primer will introduce an established set of personal training principles developed for high-level athletes that are equally applicable to police training.

Reality Check

The training approach presented in this primer is based on some fundamental realities. The following tough questions illuminate the human and financial limitations that all trainers must face:

Who are we training?

Every person joining the police force has certain strengths and weaknesses. Not everyone will learn the new skill sets presented in training at the same rate, something that many trainers ignore. Officers come from a variety of backgrounds, ages, experiences, and abilities, and are hired on the basis of a variety of competencies such as conflict management, integrity, values, decision-making ability, education, or any number of human resources mandates. However, I can promise you that tactical aptitude will never be on the list of recruiting and hiring criteria. Trainers must accept this reality and design their curriculum so that every student has an equal opportunity to learn the skills needed to be adept at tactics.

How long do we have to train them?

Law enforcement organizations in North America are generous if they give their members one full day per year to use of force/defensive tactics recertification training. Eight hours every two years is more likely. The Commission on Accreditation for Law Enforcement Agencies (CALEA) mandates how much training organizations must provide to members that bare the coveted gold sticker on their marked police units. Yet CALEA does not even specify the number of hours required to meet its *gold standard* in the use of force/defensive tactics training, only that it can be done through a variety of delivery methods. Given this *check-in-the-box* methodology, it's hard to see officer safety and defensive tactics training as a high priority for anyone—except for frontline officers and their families, that is. In the average eight-hour period allotted for training, instructors are required to teach not only basic training topics such as handcuffing, using the baton, oleoresin capsicum, and so on, but also political knee jerk reaction topics such as the current de-escalation techniques. Trainers are crippled by time constraints while being obligated to deliver training to satisfy political agendas. Training that genuinely enhances officer safety often gets neglected.

The reality is that we have very little time to deliver our training. This is one reason why a formation training system needs to be as simple as possible if students are to stand any chance of retaining it and using it in the field.

How often do officers continue to train after they leave the training program?

Look at your own organization and you will see that the unfortunate answer to this question is "not at all," or "when they have to." With all the stressors an officer needs to deal with in the field and all the challenges our profession places on families and individuals, it's no surprise that our members don't seek out additional training opportunities. Also, police organizations are similar in structure to corporate financial organizations. People hours equal money, thus every hour of an officer's time has a dollar figure associated to it. Police services are very unlikely to use money from other parts of their budget on additional training, even if that training is for officer safety. This will likely never change, so the prudent trainer should accept this reality and construct simple programs that with frequent repetitions have the highest chance of transferring to the field.

These are the realities all police trainers need to face. Our honest acceptance of these points should moderate our expectations of our students and programs. All too often, bright training minds construct exceptional programs and systems that look flawless on the drawing board and can even be executed in the training environment, but have not been designed with these three realities in mind.

Additionally, training programs are not always designed to compensate for *skills erosion*. Skills are perishable and will become less effective if not used. This primer will help you train officers in tactics that are less susceptible to erosion; it will also show you a technique to decrease the erosion of your collective hard-earned training results after students leave your training environment. The best formation with the highest likelihood of retention and success in the field will be the single, simple formation steeped in sound principles.

Probabilities versus Possibilities

Further to the these three realities and skills erosion, curriculums need to distinguish between *probabilities* and *possibilities*. We can't use training time to create complex solutions to situations that are possible but not likely to occur, if at all. I have yet to participate in a training day that has not become bogged down in the *tactical debate*. This usually begins with a "what if" scenario-based question to determine what tactic would be best for a specific scenario— for example, in a room-clearing situation. From this, the discussion morphs into an egotistically fuelled debate during which treasured training time is squandered. Perhaps a dedicated tactical unit may have the time or the need to create tailored solutions to more challenging problems, but uniformed operations must focus on best practices for the most likely situations.

By resorting to our principles as a tactical tool box, we can construct a best practice for the highest probabilities and avoid getting mired down in debate looking for perfect solutions. I believe there is great advantage to aggressiveness and decisiveness and agree with General Douglas MacArthur when he said: *"Have a good plan, execute it violently, and do it today."* The perfect plan is seldom attainable.

All these components—simplicity, reality, flexibility, rules of thumb, consistent communication, and focusing on the most likely probabilities—are essential and will be given their due in this training primer. By using this approach to training, not only will we construct a single formation for the highest chance of success in the most likely situations, but we will also further our understanding of truths and principles that will enhance the effectiveness of all the programs in our police training curriculum.

As chapters 5–7 will show, these elements come together in constructing a single formation, made up of team members who have learned to adapt from a slow and methodical building search to dealing with an active killer in process and back again. I draw upon the most prominent research into active killings in the United States to validate this system of formation training. The results of this research I'm referencing should have readers reconsidering the training systems they have employed until now.

A single flexible formation can only be achieved once the principles, rules of thumb, and practical realities are integrated into the system. Officers need to learn a basic formation system, but more importantly, they need to internalize the principles behind this system and be able to adapt them to changing tactical objectives rather than assuming a different formation for each new situation.

In order for this to happen, we need **to train the brain**. That is to say, we trainers need to teach our students how to think rather than just giving them a handful of specific solutions to a handful of specific problems. Our students need to be problem solvers. This primer will serve as a means of empowering your students to solve problems in a tactically sound manner and will likely provide a fresh perspective and review for trainers as well.

Using this primer, your officers will learn one formation, but more than just a physical skill set, they will adopt a tactically sound mind-set and attitude. They will possess the techniques and understanding to adapt effectively to every situation and changing environment. The training focus becomes how to attend to the objective, recognize the threat, and apply principles, not a navigation of chalkboard debates.

The result is a moving, shape-changing mass of tactically sound, principle-based organisms, each communicating verbally and nonverbally with each other, making safe decisions in harmony with their ever-changing mission and environment.

Like an amoeba.

2
Principles

Advanced techniques are the basics mastered.
 Samurai maxim

Principles are the foundation on which our tactics are built. A principle is a comprehensive and fundamental law, doctrine, or assumption. This training primer begins with an in-depth discussion of principles, because for a single formation to be successful in the highest number of situations, each member of that formation must have an intrinsic working knowledge of these principles.

All the members of a tactical formation need to understand *why they are doing what they are doing,* and apply these principles with little time to think. In a static environment, officers can be taught to conduct a tactical building search, with proficiency, in a very short time. But when things turn out to be not as expected, when officers need to make a quick decision to adjust to a specific problem that they have not trained for, with no instructor present to tell them what to do-when all hell breaks loose- this is when the depth of an officer's skill level and understanding, or lack thereof, becomes apparent.

When problematic scenarios such as these are raised during training, typically trainers will go back to the drawing board, or worse, stop training and debate the best solution to the dilemma. Quite often, these debates will take time to resolve at the expense of valuable practice time.

Trainers should take solace in knowing that there will rarely, if ever, be enough training time to construct an effective solution to every problem that officers might discover, and even if this were possible, there would not be time to train officers with the number of repetitions required to perform those tactics in the field. This is why a principle-based approach has the most value. As trainers, we need to instil principles that will enable our officers to make tactically sound decisions and deal independently with unexpected situations in a timely manner.

Our principle-based training starts with an exploration of some pioneers of critical thinking who analyzed exactly *why we do what we do*. As we explore these concepts, pay attention to the rules of thumb **in bold**. These act as another layer of insulation to safeguard the steadfastness of our practices.

The OODA Loop

Sun Tzu's *The Art of War* (ca. 6th century) is one of the earliest known writings on the principles of strategy and war. Although it is considered one of the finest doctrines on military strategy ever composed, Sun Tzu's focus was on macro philosophies, and the treatise offers little by way of individual tactics.

A more specific—and much more recent—approach to military tactics that has been recognized by the law enforcement community is the **OODA Loop**. An acronym for observe–orient–decide–act, the OODA Loop was developed in the 1960s by United States Air Force Pilot Colonel John Boyd. Boyd, who had degrees in economics and industrial engineering, applied his higher education and logical thinking to the realm of tactics. In formulating his decision-making cycle, he drew from a variety of scientific theories.

Essentially, the OODA Loop is premised on the idea that we are in a constant state of uncertainty and therefore rely on mental models to help us make sense and order of our experiences. Mental models are patterns our brains have learned to follow. Sometimes these are referred to as schemas or hardwiring, where neurons firing repeatedly will form pathways in our brain. These pathways are physically set and reinforced within our brain tissues, hence the term "hardwired," making the same actions easier to access in the future.

Models can be very useful if they work, but if they don't, they can be counterproductive. If a mental model we are depending on doesn't work, then it needs to be deconstructed and reconstructed. If we are not able to do this, or if we are relying too much on old models that have given us success in the past but are not working now, or if our adversary is able to deconstruct and reconstruct mental models better than we can, we will not succeed.

Using the OODA Loop can help us determine exactly what we need to do better than our adversary in order to gain the upper hand. The stages are all interdependent and continually changing; thus the loop is not a checklist but a process or continuous cycle (see figure).

Let's break it down.

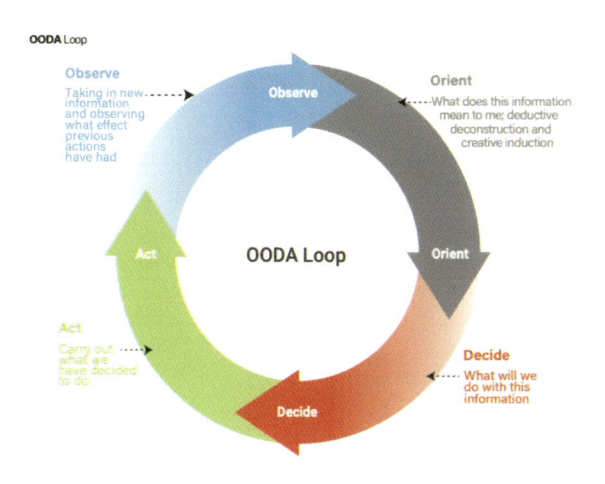

OODA Loop

Observe
Taking in new information and observing what effect previous actions have had

Orient
What does this information mean to me; deductive deconstruction and creative induction

Decide
What will we do with this information

Act
Carry out what we have decided to do

The OODA Loop

Observe

This is the stage of being aware of our surroundings and continually taking in new information. Knowledge is power, but it is not always the person with the most information who will hold the advantage, but the one who processes that information best. Therefore, the observation stage is not only about taking in information but also about how we filter and perceive that information, that is, how it relates to the unfolding circumstances and what context it has for us. The observation stage comes naturally to police officers, as we are constantly in a state of observing.

Orient

This stage consists of orienting ourselves physically and mentally to a potential threat. This is the "*what does this information mean to us*" stage. The orientation stage is where our mental models exist: it's where we construct our beliefs, based on past experiences and existing models. Boyd called this continual process of breaking down models and putting them back together "deductive deconstruction" and "creative induction." According to him, whoever does this best will have the initiative. Proper training helps us to construct mental models or reconstruct existing mental models successfully to succeed over our adversary.

Decide

In this stage we decide which action is best and what effect it will have on the situation. What we decide will depend not only on things learned in the observation and orientation phases but also on our training. Much of this stage can be preconstructed in training. We need to develop as many effective models as possible beforehand so that new models do not need to be created for each new scenario. This frees up our brains to assess which model or action will be appropriate. This is how proper training can make the OODA process more efficient—the well-trained officer already knows how to execute prescribed physical actions, given certain stimuli.

Act

The action stage is where we follow through with our decision and find out what works. How have our observations, orientation, and decision on which action to take effected the unfolding circumstances? If we observe our actions to be successful then we will achieve our intended result, but if we observe they are not, we must reorient and reconstruct our model to cope with the change. If we are unable to do that, if we have not constructed effective models beforehand, or if our adversaries are better at deconstructing and reconstructing their models, we will lose.

Sometimes, we will act only to elicit a specific and predictable reaction from our adversary in order to follow through with a second action planned for this reaction. In the combative sport of judo, this is called *kuzushi*. *Kuzushi* comes from the Japanese verb meaning to level, put down, destroy, or demolish. As a strategy in judo, *kuzushi* is employed by the skilled judo fighter (judoka) to place an opponent off-balance. By attacking with a feigned throw, the opponent will defend in a predictable manner and be set up in precisely the way the attacker predicted. Having an opponent off-balance is the only advantage the skilled judoka needs to execute a previously perfected (through proper training) finishing throw. *Ippon!*

In reality this equates to life and death.

Extremely skilled strategists will be several (OODA) loops ahead of their opponent, as we see often in a chess match. These strategists are masters of the OODA Loop.

Police officers can be masters of the OODA Loop as well. If we are acting according to principles and in a tactically sound manner, drawing on our training and planning properly, we should be successful given these advantages and others we have over an adversary, such as weapon options, additional personnel, and intelligence. For example, if officers encounter a threat, they will have a lethal force option (plan A). Observation, however, may lead them to decide that lethal force is not the appropriate action. This is a foreseeable issue, so officers will have already anticipated a secondary action such as a less lethal option to use (plan B). And if plan B doesn't work or is not required, then plan C, and so on. This is exactly how good tactics are born—by planning for situations, by processing the OODA Loop ahead of time, and also by constructing other models in case the one we first constructed does not work. By planning for the possibility that the first option may be unsuccessful and creating a second option, officers have already oriented themselves and decided more effectively than their adversary, before the engagement has even occurred. And by having already decided what actions they are going to take, thanks to effective training, they can move more quickly through the orientation and decision stages.

Nowadays, it is necessary for officers to have a lethal and less lethal option to use, but there was a time when it was not usual. This is how good principles generate good tactics. The first officers who learned it was best to have a backup plan in case the first choice didn't work were adhering to Boyd's theory of deconstructing and reconstructing mental models, whether they were aware of it or not.

By realizing that we may not be able to reconstruct our mental models in enough time or that the consequences are too grave to risk it, we plan for these adversities. Most times our opponents don't plan, or *we take away their time to plan*. By understanding the human mental process, we can construct appropriate and effective models before our adversary does. We win by using the human process to our advantage.

Let's take the OODA concept in its simplest form. We've all seen movies where the good guy is hiding from the bad guy, and the good guy throws a rock somewhere away from his position. This simple scenario demonstrates the cycle of observing, orientating, deciding, and acting. By throwing the rock, if that action is successful, the good guy has reset the bad guy's OODA Loop, requiring him to re-orient himself and decide on another action. Since the good guy has already decided what he is going to do while the bad guy is catching up, he has gained a tactical advantage.

If you think this is an oversimplification of the OODA Loop at work, then consider that one of the most commonly used strategies for gaining a tactical advantage on a high-risk entry, used by your local SWAT team as well as by special forces operators, is to throw a flash bang or distraction device into an area they plan to assault. This is the tactical equivalent of *kuzushi*. Not only have the operators created a mental stun, but they have reset, to put it mildly, the adversary's OODA Loop and created a small window of opportunity to move in and take control. Since the tactical operators know exactly what they are going to do at the sound of that flash bang and have a plan B and plan C if plan A doesn't work, all they need to do is carry out the actions. Typically—and hopefully—their adversary has not made any observations at the onset of the tactical operator's process. Now the adversary will need to re-orient and make a decision on what action to take next. By understanding and manipulating the human thought process, the tactical team has created a significant advantage. As a matter of fact, a properly planned and executed tactical assault is the paradigm of how to successfully manipulate the OODA Loop.

This is nothing new, as even an ancient proverb advises, "Make an uproar to the east and attack the west." In this primer, I will show how advanced tactics are no different in principle than these simple scenarios. Embrace that simplicity as we move forward.

By training regularly and preparing their resources effectively, officers can manipulate the OODA Loop process of their opponents and use it to great advantage. This is the essence of good tactics and can be applied to all training. Col. Boyd used his schematic to enable fighter pilots to win in air to air combat, but it is equally applicable in any combative encounter.

The Thought Process

About 25 years after Boyd created the OODA Loop, Charles Remsberg, author of the widely acknowledged Calibre Press Street Survival Series, developed a similar theory he called the **Thought Process**. Without using a detailed scientific approach, Remsberg came up with slightly different application of the same idea as Boyd's. He described the

Thought Process as a series of steps. Although this simple checklist presentation makes the Thought Process appear more user-friendly than the OODA Loop, it is crucial to remember that the steps in the Thought Process are dynamic and continually changing with each new stimulus added to the situation.

Like Boyd, Remsberg theorized that both the officer and the subject (adversary) go through stages, and whoever can do that better—not necessarily faster—wins. However, Remsberg's theory is more targeted to law enforcement, where the definition of success is different than for combatants in a military theatre, which Boyd's theory grew out of.

According to the Thought Process, an officer needs to go through the following four stages to be successful: **locate** the subject; **react** or prepare to react to the subject; **assess** or identify the threat and what an appropriate action will be, and then initiate action to **control** the subject (arrest, handcuffing, use of force) (see **Figure 2.1**). The subject or adversary only needs to **locate**, **react** to, and **attack** the officer. Because the adversary has one less step to do than the officer does, the adversary has the upper hand, which explains why officers take the precautions they do, such as using firearms readiness, tactical movement, advanced planning, and multiple force options. This is the way to level the playing field.

The Thought Process is more useful to think of as a roster of what the adversary needs to do to successfully launch an attack on us, and a corresponding roster of what we must do to thwart the attack or control the adversary. As I've stated, police officers are usually a step behind on the roster.

2:1 Thought Process

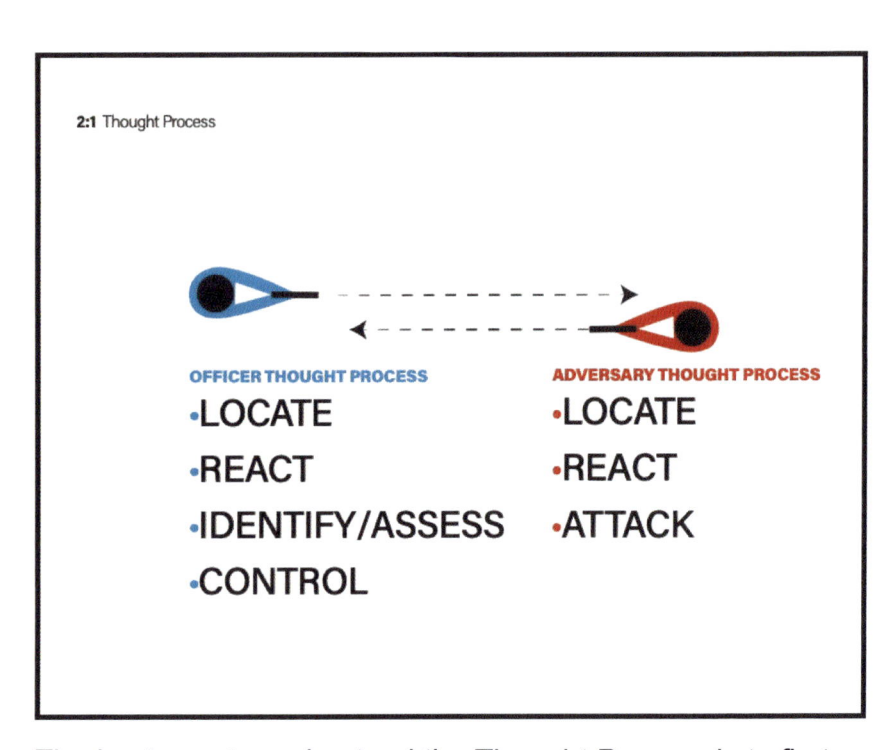

OFFICER THOUGHT PROCESS
- **LOCATE**
- **REACT**
- **IDENTIFY/ASSESS**
- **CONTROL**

ADVERSARY THOUGHT PROCESS
- **LOCATE**
- **REACT**
- **ATTACK**

The best way to understand the Thought Process is to first define each step and then discuss a *few ways* in which we can stack the deck in our favour. *The measure of good tactics will always be to shorten our Thought Process and lengthen our adversary's.* Although these steps may seem rudimentary, the value of their simplicity becomes evident when the complexity of our tactical challenges increases.

Locate

You must first locate your adversary before they locate you. Whoever is successful in first locating the other will hold a significant advantage for the remainder of the encounter, kind of like a deadly hide-and-seek game. This poses a significant disadvantage for officers, who rarely have the luxury of locating subjects before they locate us.

I remember responding to a silent break-and-enter alarm at a church early in my career. We approached with no lights or sirens so as not to give up this rare tactical advantage. We entered the church with a K-9 unit, and after a standard announcement, the handler allowed his patrol service dog to go off-leash to search for the suspect, who was located and taken into custody.

This may sound like pretty routine stuff, but after 20-plus years of service this incident still stands out for me. The reason I remember it so vividly, among the hundreds of incidents over my career, is because of how rare it is that uniformed officers "get the drop" on someone. I can count on two hands the number of times I have had the advantage of locating an adversary before they have located me as a uniformed officer.

Being able to locate the opponent before he had located us gave us a significant tactical advantage. Using superior weapons, trained personnel, and advanced planning all speak to the importance of recognizing the advantage of initiative. Most often, police officers are behind the curve. Tactical countermeasures are the way to even the score.

As an officer, you can do a variety of things to enhance your ability to locate the adversary first:

- Shine a flashlight selectively or turn on the lights in a dark room to use light to your advantage. As obvious as turning on the lights sounds, it is often overlooked. Shining light into the suspect's eyes will also take away their ability to immediately locate you.

- Secure your duty belt and keys to avoid the unnecessary noise of rattling equipment.
- When approaching a location, always consider turning off the emergency equipment and arriving undetected.
- Move through an environment, not just through doorways but around corners as well, in a smooth and methodical manner to greatly enhance your ability to locate the adversary first and put yourself in an optimal position to react effectively.

Cutting the pie is one technique for locating a suspect. This means positioning yourself as far from an edge as possible and slowly moving in a circular direction until a hiding subject can be seen (**Figure 2.2**). This enables you to observe small sections of the unknown environment incrementally and when done properly enhances your ability to locate the suspect before the suspect locates you. Cutting the pie can be executed dynamically or very slowly. It can be useful on a doorway, in rounding a hallway, or searching a closet; essentially anywhere you are moving around an edge (**Figure 2.3**).

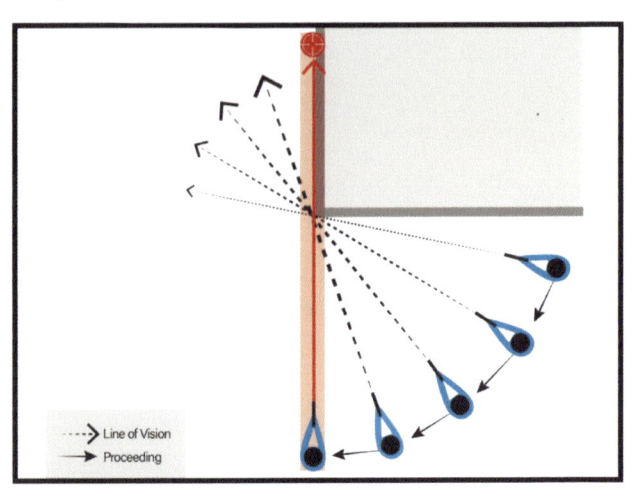

2:3 Cutting the Pie—doorway

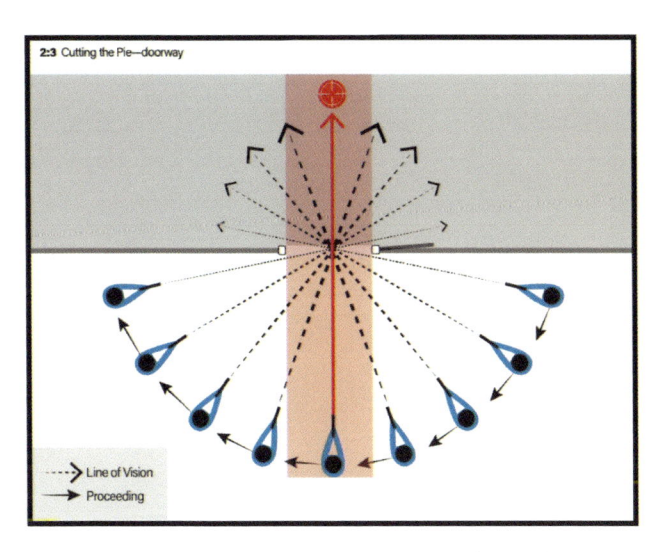

- - -> Line of Vision
——> Proceeding

Like all tactical options, cutting the pie is just that—an option. An officer must continually assess and reassess the advantages and disadvantages of any given tactic, depending on the environment or situation, they will change from moment to moment. For example, if you must place yourself in a poor tactical position by turning your back to an uncleared problem area, then cutting the pie would be a dangerous choice. In this case, you may need to change the manner in which you cut the pie and execute it dynamically (quickly) instead of statically (slowly). Again, the question of any tactic must be: *Will this enhance or shorten your thought process and hinder or lengthen that of your adversary? Will this tactic help you locate the subject before they locate you?*

I've alluded to the advantages of aggressiveness in chapter 1 and will continue to do so throughout the book; during a threshold evaluation is one of those times when we need to consider if this approach is best. As we stand outside in the hallway formulating the *perfect* plan, the subject could potentially be inside doing the same. Is it better to move with assertive authority into that room and establish a point of room domination (PRD) and position ourselves optimally to react to a threat? By moving assertively, we remove the adversary's time to think; by stalling, we give the adversary more time to formulate a plan. Every situation is different and needs to be evaluated promptly.

These are just a few ways that we can interfere with an adversary's Thought Process and, more specifically, win the contest of locating them first.

React

Reacting refers not only to the physical position in which the officer and adversary place themselves, but also to the mental component of how they are going to react to each other. The preparation for responding to the threat is almost as important as physically reacting to it.

That is why the one who is positioned and mentally prepared to react will always have a significant tactical advantage. A suspect who is trapped in a building during a police search is like a cornered animal, very dangerous and holding many tactical advantages. The officer needs to be cognizant of this and take countermeasures. Here are just a few examples:

- An officer can order a subject into a position of disadvantage. Even something as simple as having a subject facing away from you, such as when handcuffing, prevents the subject from immediately targeting you and allows you more time to process information and assess compliance.
- Smart tactics will always dictate that we **bring the subject to us**. This is one of the *rules of thumb* practiced during formation training. If you have a general idea of where the subject is, you gain a

greater advantage by commanding them out of hiding and into a known environment rather than you moving into a potential kill zone, when appropriate.
- Barriers can be a hindrance to reacting to a threat, but they can also be used to your advantage. By placing barricades between yourself and the subject, you can lengthen the amount of time it takes them to reach you and launch an attack.
- Handcuffing is undeniably the best way to reduce a subject's ability to launch an attack, but remember that a handcuffed prisoner can still be very dangerous. I have had my nose broken by a subject whose hands were cuffed behind his back. Headbutts and spitting are unpredictable and dangerous attacks, and handcuffs do nothing to hinder them.
- Mental rehearsal is another important practice that will enhance your ability to react. This is the act of pre-downloading a response from your brain. Mentally rehearsing responses to various stimuli can reduce your reaction time exponentially. I will discuss this technique in more detail later.
- Weapons readiness is critical. **The Force Science Institute** has conducted some shocking research on the realities of reaction time. For example, did you know that it takes a naive (inexperienced) shooter approximately half a second to draw a firearm from their waistband and fire at an officer, and that it would take a trained officer over twice that time to return fire from a drawn and low ready position? This research shows, among other things, the importance of weapons readiness and something as seemingly minor as maintaining a ready stance. It also shows the time lag we suffer when we're forced to

discriminate. In other words, we need to first mentally assess what we are shooting at, as opposed to the opponent, who already knows what he is going to do.

This is not an exhaustive list by any means, but serves to illustrate a few ways in which we can manipulate the Thought Process to our tactical advantage. Be mindful that your adversary can also manipulate the situation for their own advantage. The skill-less action of an adversary hiding in wait, facing the doorway with a weapon ready to use and the sound of the officers approaching puts them at a colossal advantage over you.

Tactics are a chess match, and it's not often that we police officers get to move first. Not only are we usually behind the curve, but we have an additional step to go through, as we will discuss next, which makes our process significantly more complicated than our adversary's: we need to identify what we are dealing with and assess the appropriate option.

Identify/Assess

Unlike the offender, the officer must identify and confirm the level of threat that exists in order to select an appropriate level of control, which is a complex process in itself. The officer must also assess the situation to determine whether to engage the subject or disengage.

This phase may occur simultaneously or interchangeably with the officer's reacting phase. Here's a few ways we can enhance our ability to identify or assess our adversary:

- Use time and space to improve your ability to assess and react. This distance and time will depend on your personal abilities, what weapons are being used, what barriers are in place, and of course weapons

readiness. Maintaining time and space will decrease the subject's ability to attack and increase your ability to assess and/or react.
- *Develop and maintain your weapons and skills*, as these are paramount in enhancing your abilities to deal with a threat. There will be enough unforeseeable events to deal with; the last thing you need to do is add additional challenges to the situation such as sloppy handcuffing skills or malfunctioning weapons. These issues are foreseeable and preventable. If you need to use one of your weapons, you need to be competent and capable with it. The more skilled you are with your weapons, the less likely the attacker can hurt or kill you. Maintain your weapons like they are the life-saving devices they are.
- *Use the Tactical Thinking Model*, another concept introduced by Charles Remsberg, to help make better decisions and improve your ability to assess situations. **Tactical thinking** is a way of prioritizing your focus and includes three levels. In visual terms, tactical thinking can be thought of as a target with the third level, the focal point, at the very center (**Figure 2.4**).

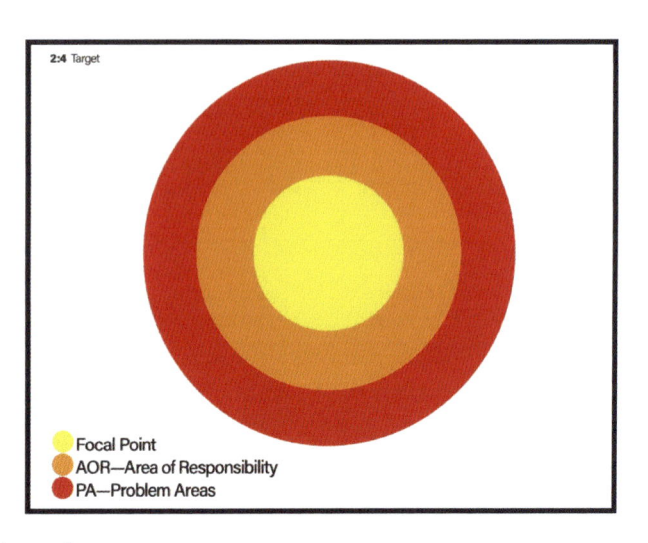

2:4 Target

- Focal Point
- AOR—Area of Responsibility
- PA—Problem Areas

Problem Area

The best way to think of a problem area is any area that has not been cleared yet (**Figure 2.5**). For the purposes of internal team movement, a problem area may be a room, gymnasium, or office space, but it could also be a hallway or tucked-away area of a room such as a closet or crawl space.

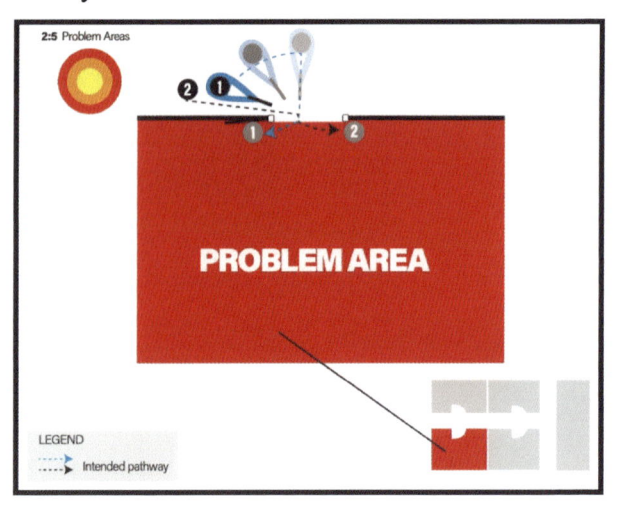

2:5 Problem Areas

LEGEND
Intended pathway

40

Area Of Responsibility

This is an area within the problem area that an individual officer is responsible for (**Figure 2.6**). If the team is moving down a hallway, officers will each assume their area of responsibility (AOR).

Sometimes an officer's AOR is understood and some times it needs to be communicated.

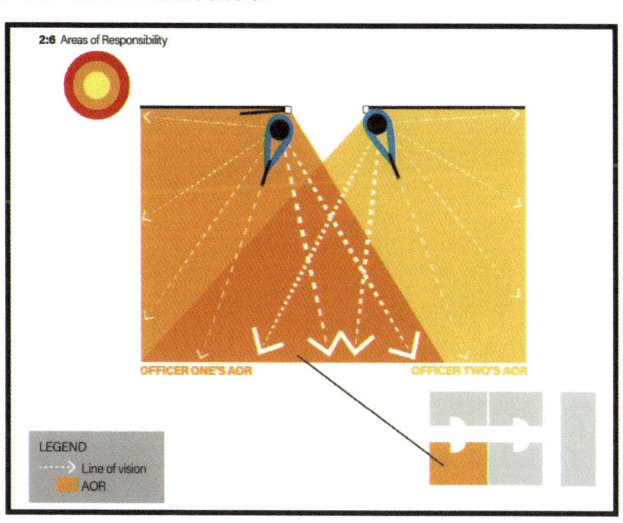

2:6 Areas of Responsibility

OFFICER ONE'S AOR   OFFICER TWO'S AOR

LEGEND
- - -> Line of vision
▨ AOR

Like a problem area, addressing AORs is a fluid process, so officers are constantly adjusting their AORs. If two officers enter a room to clear it, each assumes their AOR, as shown in **Figure 2.6**. Each officer's attention to their AOR is critical and attention should not be diverted, not even to communicate with one another.

Focal Point

The focal point is a clear and present threat that must be controlled immediately. It is usually a person. If a threat

2:7

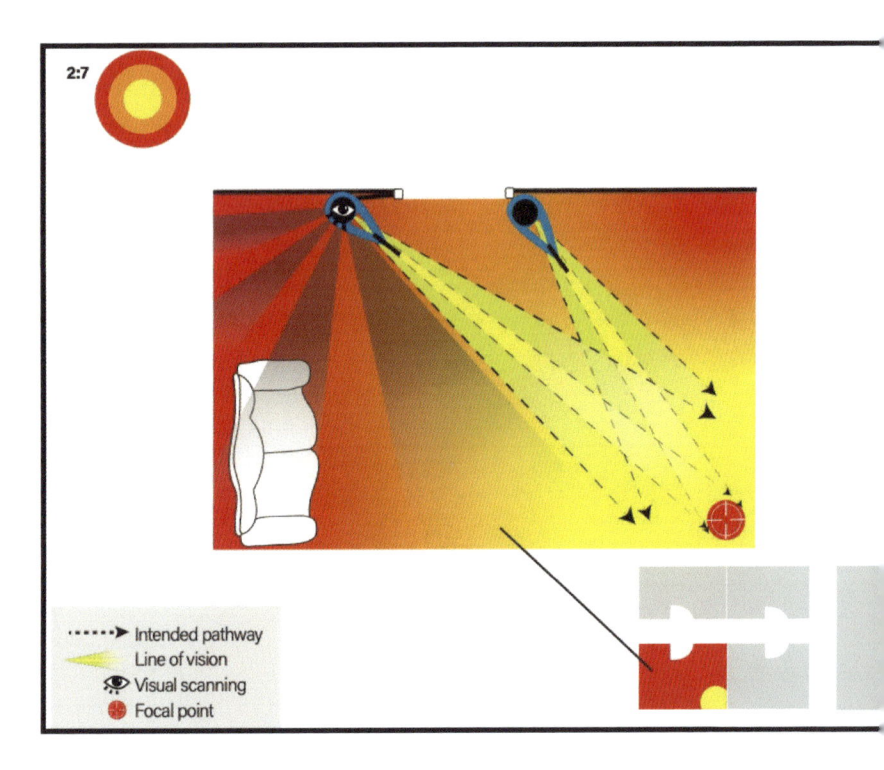

- ┈┈▶ Intended pathway
- Line of vision
- Visual scanning
- Focal point

emerges when officers are moving through a problem area, it must be given the highest priority.

If a threat emanates in the problem area before the area is cleared, as is often the case, officers will give the threat priority but must never forget that there are still uncleared problem areas (**Figure 2.7**). Officers will have to decide whether to control the subject first or to clear the area first and then control the subject. Depending on the circumstances, either is correct. If the subject is compliant and the officers have placed them in a position of disadvantage, such as proning them out, the officers may choose to clear the problem area first, or they may attend to

42

the threat first. That is their judgment call to make, based on their perceptions.

If the subject is combative, officers must attend to that threat, as **a real threat always takes priority over a perceived threat**. However, uncleared problem areas must never be neglected. I will discuss ways such as visual scanning to deal with this effectively.

Attack versus Control

This is the final stage of the Thought Process. The adversary only needs to carry out the physical action of attacking, which they likely have already predetermined. But for the officer it is not as easy. As an officer, you need to assess what type of control is necessary, which is a complex process in itself. Once you have made an observation, you are not justified in simply attacking your adversary—you must restrain them and take them into custody, using only the amount of force that is subjectively and objectively deemed reasonable and necessary under the circumstances. Attacking would be much easier. As a matter of fact, the whole Thought Process seems to favour the adversary. However, there are many things you can do to tip the odds back in your favour. This part of the Thought Process demonstrates the importance of understanding the totality of circumstances you are in and using any and all of the resources available to you to win.

As both the OODA Loop and Thought Process demonstrate, your goal as a police officer is always to maximize or lengthen the thought process of your subject and minimize or shorten your own. Contemplate a few of the ways in which you can practice this, not only in your tactical formation training but in all areas of your training curriculum. Being able to shorten your thought process while lengthening that of your opponent's will be the ultimate litmus test of the tactics you employ. Taking time to discuss principles like the OODA Loop and the Thought Process is important, because as we move into tactical formation training, these principles become the *answer key.* There is no possible way, given the training limitations and realities we are challenged with, that we can tailor a specific response to each situation. The only way to succeed as police officers is to have an intrinsic understanding of these principles so we can adjust to the unplanned challenges and respond with tactically sound decisions.

These concepts and techniques may sound simple, but when situations become complex, it's the simple techniques that we always count on, like an old friend. One of my favourite sayings is a samurai maxim: "Advanced techniques are the basics mastered." The OODA Loop and the Thought Process are the basics that we must master.

Remsberg and Boyd were tactical thinking pioneers who recognized the importance of gaining and maintaining initiative during combative encounters, as well as in the time-sensitive processes that shape our tactics. The thought processes they've identified serve as a higher criteria for the operating tactics we employ.

Sound principles give us an anchor point for asking the right questions about our tactics. For example, using the OODA Loop we can ask: Will this tactic allow us to observe–orient–decide–act better and faster than our adversary? If the answer is yes, the tactic is sound; if the answer is no, it is not. Consider the OODA Loop and the Thought Process to be your starting points from which to determine which tactics are optimal for a situation.

For the single flexible formation proposed in this training primer to work, not only will you need to understand where good tactics come from so that you can create sound solutions, but if you are a trainer you will also have to teach your students how to create sound solutions on their own. Principle-based thinking such as the Thought Process and the OODA Loop begets sound tactics.

In the following chapters I will refer most frequently to the Thought Process, because that is the theory I am most familiar with. However, I strongly encourage you to become intimately familiar with both the Thought Process and the OODA Loop.

3
Communication

*Strategy without tactics is the slowest route to victory.
Tactics without strategy is the noise before defeat.
Sun Tzu, The Art of War*

For the single flexible formation to be successful, its members need to be able to communicate with each other in simple language. In this chapter, I will introduce a basic set of verbal and non-verbal communications. Verbal commands enable team members to relay to each other what their intentions are so they can clear their AORs as efficiently and safely as possible. These commands are typically announced by the lead officer, who will usually be the one making the next tactical decision or movement. However, non-verbal forms of communication such as reading off and squeezing up are equally, if not more important, especially for team members following the lead officer.

I will first introduce the verbal commands and then move on to non-verbal techniques.

Verbal Commands

The following commands are commonly used by officers in tactical formations during internal team movement .

"Door" (left, right, straight, open, or closed)

This command is used by the lead officer to announce that he is staging at a doorway he plans to enter. The purpose of the officer announcing the door he plans to enter is to inform the officer/s behind him of his intentions, as he will need their support.

When the lead officer observes a door he plans to enter, he will stop a distance away from the entrance so that he cannot be seen from inside by a potential threat. This is when he announces his intention to enter that room by stating "door right," "door straight," or "door left" (**Figure 3.1**). At least two officers will enter a room, unless that is not possible.

The lead officer waits for the trailing officer to *squeeze up* (see non-verbal communication), giving him the assurance he needs before entering the room that he will not be doing so alone. Once he receives this assurance, he will make his threshold evaluation and enter the room.

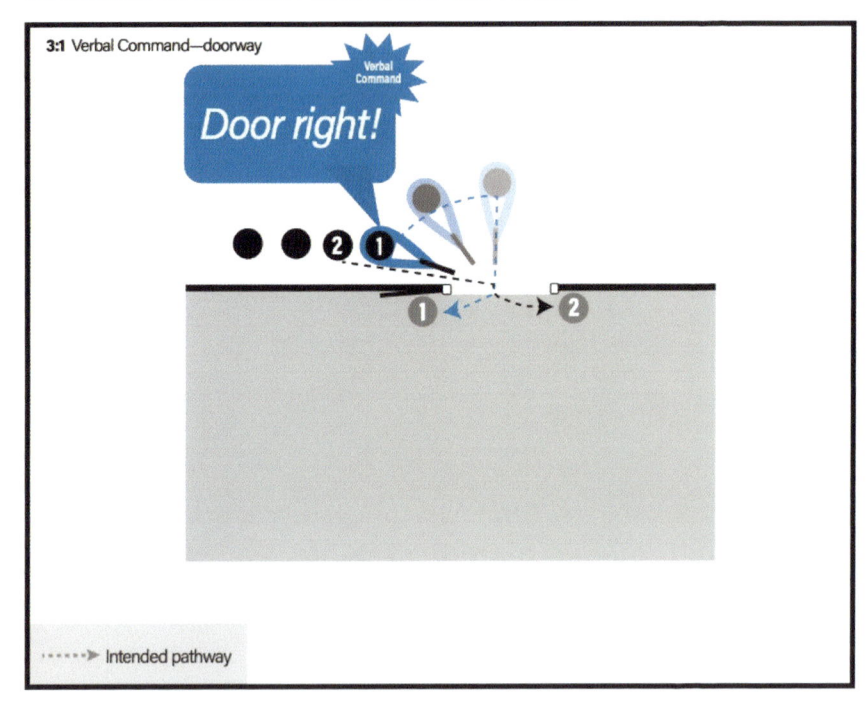

3:1 Verbal Command—doorway

Door right!

Verbal Command

······▶ Intended pathway

The lead officer may or may not announce that the door is open or closed, depending on whether he feels that it is something that the trailing officer/s needs to know. For example, if the officer stages on a closed door, he may opt to open that door while conducting his threshold evaluation. This would be beneficial for the trailing officer to know.

A lead officer may also choose to announce if a door is outward opening or inward opening. An outward-opening door in an interior residential setting often indicates a closet or bathroom. Announcing that the door is outward opening may better prepare the trailing officer so that he doesn't bump into the lead officer, or for the possibility that the room will be small. Since inward-opening doors are more common, a door is usually assumed to be such unless otherwise specified.

"Small room"

This is announced by the lead officer entering a room to signify that the room is too small for another officer, or that she doesn't require assistance clearing that room. "Small room" may be announced as the officer enters a closet or small bathroom, for example, or before entering

the room (**Figure 3.2**). By announcing a small room, the lead officer signifies that she does not need to be followed into that room. The trailing officer will then become the lead officer, stand by in case required or fall in formation behind other officers.

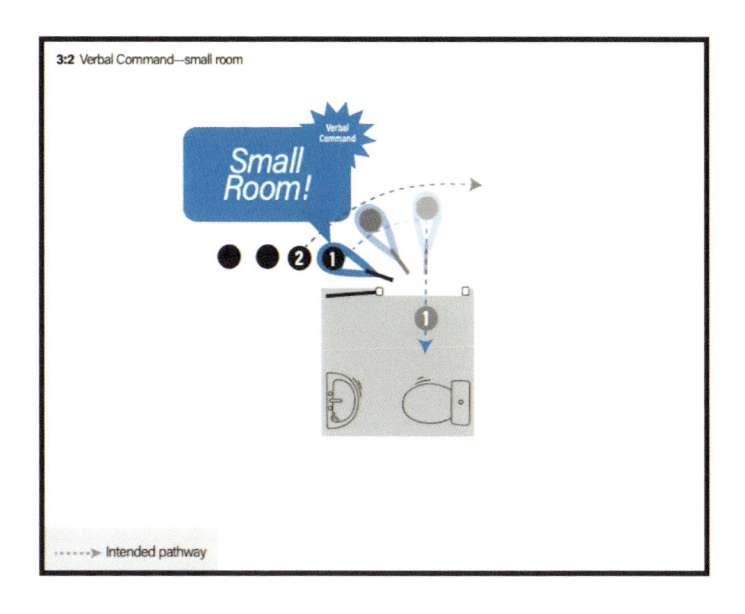

3:2 Verbal Command—small room

·····▶ Intended pathway

3:3 Posting

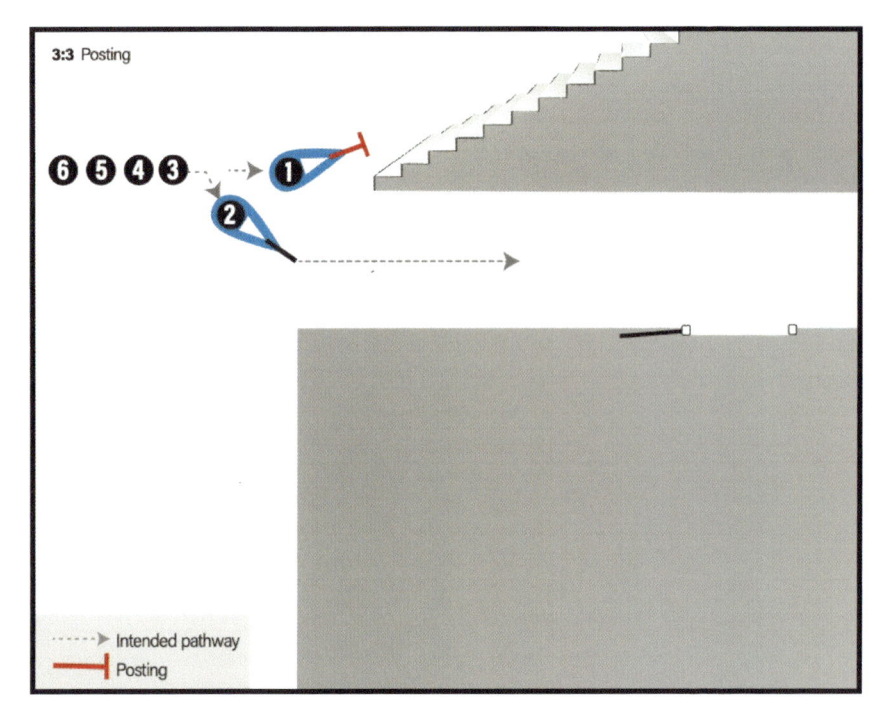

"Posting" (left, right, straight ahead, stairs, etc.)

"Posting" is the command used by an officer, usually the lead officer, to announce that he will be stopping and covering a designated area. Posting is crucial if officers are passing an area that may pose a threat but is not the highest priority at that moment.

For example, quite often entries will be intelligence driven. Officers may receive information that the target of their investigation is on the main floor. The officers will want to reach that target as quickly as possible, but they cannot leave problem areas uncovered. This is when an officer will either assign himself or be assigned to post on areas such as the upstairs or downstairs (**Figure 3.3**). The posting officer will remain in place and focused on his AOR until joined by the other officers. At that time, officers will proceed together to clear the remaining areas that were posted upon.

"Blue on blue"

This announcement is used by officers when they have contact with other officers (**Figure 3.4**). The "blue on blue" command is not used every time there is officer-to-officer contact but only when there is a potential for confusion, to avoid mistaking another officer for a potential adversary.

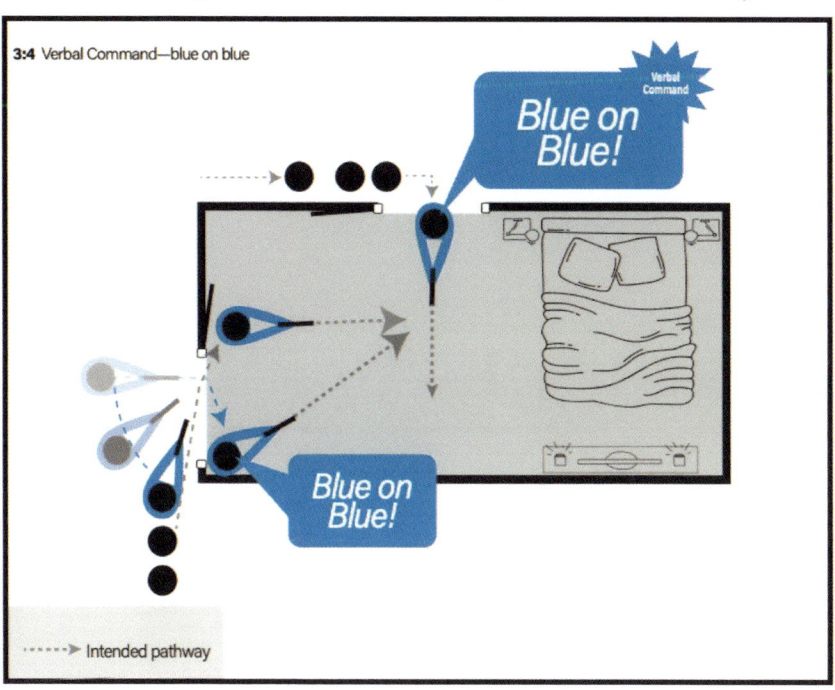

3:4 Verbal Command—blue on blue

"Looking for work"

This command is used by officers who are rejoining other officers in a search effort but are unsure of what has and has not been cleared. This is a common problem and for that reason, often one person, such as the team leader or supervisor, will remain independent of the search effort to maintain oversight of the situation. The "looking for work" command should only be used when officers are looking for direction.

"Trailers"

This command is used by officers to request more personnel at their location. More officers may be needed to assist in handling subjects or clearing large areas.

"Covering"

The officer who announces "covering" is indicating that she is concentrating solely on watching for threats in her AOR that may expose her partner to danger (**Figure 3.5**).

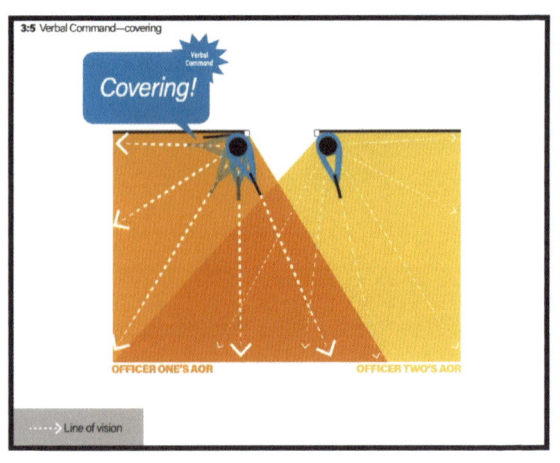

3:5 Verbal Command—covering

"Searching"

The officer who announces that she is "searching" is indicating to her partner that she is moving into their AOR and searching for threats (**Figure 3.6**). An officer will only announce "searching" after she has heard her partner announce "covering."

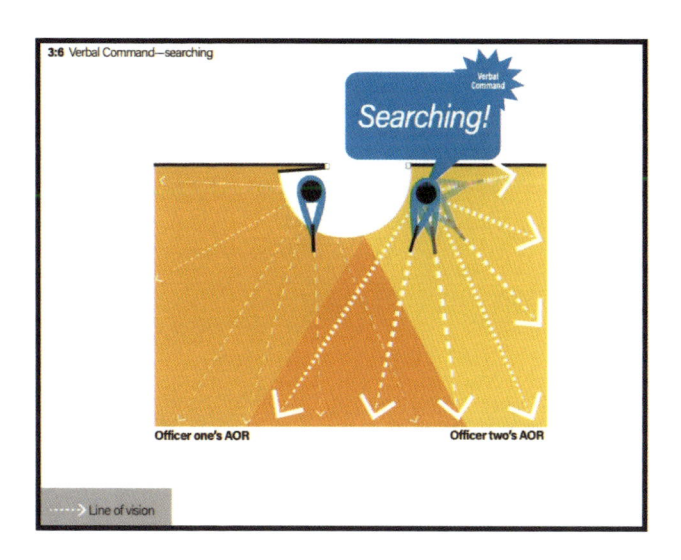

3:6 Verbal Command—searching

"Clear"

"Clear" is announced only once officers have completed their search of a room or area and it is in fact clear. This term should not be used hastily. This also serves as notice to other officers that an area has been searched.

"Coming out"

When an officer is exiting a cleared area, "coming out" is announced in order to avoid startling other officers. This also signifies to a supervisor that the officer may be seeking direction.

"Who's with me?"

The officer who announces this has staged on and called the door or area he intends to enter but has not yet felt a squeeze up (later in this chapter) from another accompanying officer. The "who's with me?" command is important to clarify that an officer will not be going into a room by himself and needs to wait for additional resources; it also serves as a reminder to a trailing officer who has forgotten to squeeze up. An officer should never neglect his AOR and turn around to look for somebody to issue this or any other verbal command.

Non-verbal Communication

Reading Off

Reading off, or sometimes referred to as **keying off,** means that an officer's tactical movement is dictated by another officer, most often but not necessarily the one in front. When the lead officer stages on a doorway and announces the intention to enter a room, the officer behind her needs to read off that lead officer's movement.

If the lead officer posts on a hallway, the trailing officer will still read off her movement, but now the trailing officer will become the lead officer because he understands that posting is usually a single-officer job. It is the responsibility of the trailing officer to read, without fail, the actions of the officer directly in front.

Reading off binds the formation together. If you are the lead officer, then the team is yours to take where you see fit. This is why it is imperative that each member of the formation is sufficiently skilled in the tactical principles we've discussed, because the lead officer will constantly be changing.

If the lead officer stages on a door, for example, she will announce her intentions to enter that room and the person behind her will be reading off her movement. However, if the lead officer posts on a stairwell, the trailing officer will recognize that posting only requires one person and now take the role of lead officer. Reading off is an incredibly flexible, multi-use tool that we will be revisiting often in this primer as it is critical to the success of the single formation.

Reading off also applies to room entries. Since the configuration of a room should never be assumed, even with reliable intelligence, officers cannot rely on predetermined movement such as criss-crossing or button hooks. Instead, officers need to read off each other's movements. This practice allows proper tactical movement regardless of the interior configuration in the room or area being infiltrated.

Since the second officer always reads off the movement of the lead officer, the lead officer must make her movements obvious and dedicated. If the lead officer is hesitant, it is harder for the second officer to read off her movement. The front officer must ensure that she enters the room with a commitment to create room for the second officer's entry. If the lead officer fails to enter the room completely, the second officer will be jammed up in the doorway, creating a significant safety risk. Furthermore, if officers are stalled in the doorway, it will hinder their ability to disengage from the room if they need to. The exception to this would be if the leading officer encounters a situation that would put her in imminent danger to proceed.

Perhaps the most valuable attribute of reading off is that it acts as a built-in corrector. This is extremely important to have, because mistakes happen. If there isn't a means of correcting mistakes on the fly, the formation falls apart and the advantage goes to our adversaries. I will demonstrate the ways that reading off corrects mistakes in chapter 6.

Squeezing Up

Squeezing up provides a nonverbal assurance to an officer that he will not be entering a room or an area, and possibly a threatening situation, by himself. The trailing officer squeezes the shoulder or other designated area of the officer in front. This is typically done when staging at a doorway but is useful in other situations as well. The reason an officer will squeeze instead of tap is to avoid unintentionally giving his partner the message that he is ready to enter a room or breach a threshold when he is not. Furthermore, the squeeze is an emotional reassurance to your teammates that you will not be going into a dangerous situation alone.

The communication strategies introduced in this chapter are only a basic set of verbal commands that are widely used, along with some non-verbal strategies that will reduce confusion and mitigate errors. As you practice these techniques, try not to get caught up in semantic details, as it is far more important to use simple and consistent language within your units and organizations than to be concerned about which words are used.

4

Training Humans

*Moving, be like water.
Still, be like a mirror.
Respond, like an echo.
Bruce Lee, Tao of Jeet Kune Do*

As police trainers, we need to be reminded from time to time that we're working with human beings, not programming computers. Any lesson in defensive tactics would be remiss if it didn't take time to review some of the physiological factors that will affect performance during periods of stress. Bruce Siddle and his organization, Pressure Point Control Tactics (PPCT), have contributed an admirable amount of research to what law enforcement professionals do. Much of the information in this chapter is the result of their hard work.

In his book *Sharpening the Warrior's Edge*, Siddle defined the term **survival stress** as "a deadly force threat perception that initiates the sympathetic nervous system discharge." I emphasize *perception*, because how we perceive the level of threat influences the stress response we will have to it.

Survival Stress and Motor Skills

The activation of your **sympathetic nervous system** (**SNS**), more commonly know as the fight-or-flight response, is designed to help you survive. This activation increases muscle blood flow and tension, dilates pupils, and accelerates heart rate and respiration.

SNS activation is the body's way of preparing you to face or escape from an acutely stressful encounter. A stressful situation can trigger a dump of stress hormones that produce well-orchestrated physiological changes. Although some of the effects of these hormones are positive, as we will discuss, they also present unique challenges that are very important for us to understand. Due to vasoconstriction, which is a narrowing or tightening of the blood vessels, we experience changes to our motor skill performance. Let's break it down further. The PPCT's *Defensive Tactics*

Instructor Manual describes the following three types motor skills.

Fine Motor Skills

These are "skills that require hand-eye coordination and dexterity. When the heart rate reaches around 115 bpm, the effects of vasoconstriction to the fingers and hands diminish the dexterity required to perform fine motor skills." Handwriting is a prime example of a fine motor skill. If you've ever been trembling and found it hard to write down information after a traffic collision, you've experienced this effect. Of more relevance to us, precision shooting is a fine motor skill.

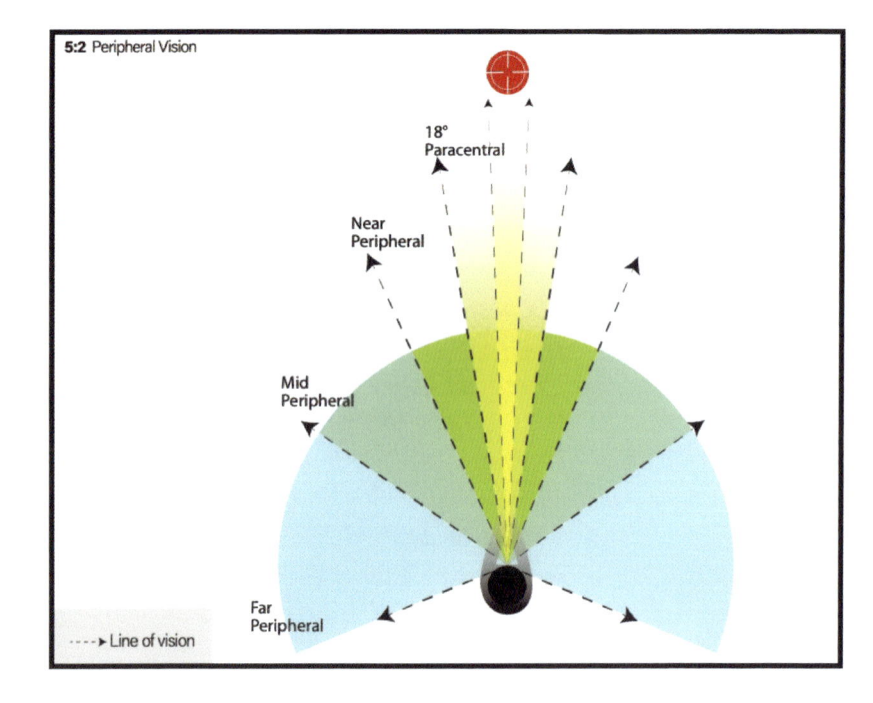

5:2 Peripheral Vision

- 18° Paracentral
- Near Peripheral
- Mid Peripheral
- Far Peripheral
- ---▶ Line of vision

Complex Motor Skills

Complex motor skills involve a "series of muscle groups or movements requiring hand-eye coordination, precision, tracking, and timing." At a heart rate of approximately 145 bpm (beats per minute), complex motor skills begin to deteriorate. A defensive tactics technique that has multiple independent components, such as an arm bar takedown, is an example of a complex motor skill.

Gross Motor Skills

These are skills that involve "large muscles or major muscle groups." Gross motor skills are simple strength skills or skills involving symmetrical movements. A straight punch, a squat, running, or jumping are all gross motor skills. This is the only type of motor skill that becomes more effective when your SNS-activated heart rate increases.

To summarize, with the increased heart rate that accompanies SNS activation comes a deterioration of fine and complex motor skills and an enhancement of gross motor skills. Note that these effects are related to *hormonally* induced heart-rate increases. An increased heart rate caused by physical exercise, such as wind sprints, will not have the same impact. I've personally observed the monitored heart rates of extremely fit recruits participating in stressful dynamic scenarios training jump from 80 to 200 bpm in five seconds. There is no exercise that can replicate that. As a matter of fact, high level athletes who train regularly can achieve *greater* performance outcomes with an increased heart rate. For trainers, this is important to remember if elevating the heart rates of your students through exercise is a means you use to replicate a stress response in your training. Keep in mind that this manufactured stress will not replicate the acute stress of a life-and-death encounter.

Survival Stress and the Senses

In addition to affecting motor skills performance, survival stress also has a significant impact on the senses. Each of the five sensory systems, also referred to as the perceptual senses, provides the brain with a constant flow of information. However, when you focus on a particular activity or threat, your brain will tune in to the sensory system that provides the most relevant information at that given second. All other sensory inputs will be tuned out by the brain because they lack immediate significance. This is a phenomenon referred to as perceptual narrowing or selective attention. Here are a few examples as described by the *PPCT Defensive Tactics Instructor Manual,* and their implications for formation training

Auditory Exclusion

In survival stress situations, **auditory exclusion** can "significantly limit an officer's ability in survival stress situations to process critical information." Verbal commands, information shouted by another officer, or even shouts of surrender from a suspect may go unheard due to auditory exclusion. For this reason, in a stressful building search or dynamic entry situation, verbal commands should be concise, consistent, loud, repetitive, and clear.

An important thing to remember is that the suspect may also be experiencing these effects. Officers need to consider that a suspect's less-than-immediate compliance may be a result of their own survival stress, and not necessarily a sign of resistive behaviour.

Visual Effects

Usually vision is the dominant source of information to the brain. However, when the auditory system is the dominant source of information, such as in low or no-light environments, **visual exclusion** may occur. The following are other examples of visual perceptual narrowing.

Tunnel Vision

Tunnel vision is a phenomenon in which your vision literally narrows, as though you were "looking through a tunnel or a tube, with a reduction of 70% or more of the peripheral field." Tunnel vision is without question the greatest threat to conducting building searches effectively because of our reliance on peripheral vision. I'll introduce a coping mechanism near the end of the chapter, under *scanning*.

Loss of Near Vision

"When near vision loss occurs, you experience great difficulty focusing on objects closer than four feet. This is caused by pupil dilation, which is a byproduct of SNS activation. When the pupils dilate, the ability to focus on the sights on a firearm or on close threats and visual cues is compromised."

Loss of Ability to Visually Focus

"Excitement of the SNS causes relaxation and loss of control over the muscles that control the eye's lens, which distorts a target when you try to focus on it." Thus, even the small amount of sensory information being processed by the brain is flawed, causing a significant decrease in your accuracy skills and a significant increase in reaction time.

Loss of Monocular Vision

Monocular (one-eyed) vision is "predominantly used in shooting situations where accuracy is critical, but because of the SNS activation, it's one of the first things to be affected." Being aware of this means we should incorporate more reflexing shooting platforms and rely less on aimed fire when conducting building searches.

Loss of Depth Perception

"Loss of depth perception will cause you to incorrectly estimate distance." Since it's in your body's best interest to survive, this might tell you that dangerous things are closer than they actually are. When our ancestors' brains told them the dangerous mammoth charging at them was closer than it really was, this allowed them time to escape—otherwise, we humans would probably be extinct. This, along with other physiological effects of stress, are the body's attempts to enhance our chances of survival. However, modern day training programs must recognize this potential for misperception when designing curriculum.

Loss of Night Vision

"The night vision receptors in your eye are located primarily in the peripheral field. Loss of the peripheral field due to tunnel vision will also result in a loss of night vision." This should prompt us to use light to our greatest tactical advantage and adopt some of the strategies to manage stress discussed later in this chapter when conducting building searches in low light conditions.

Managing Stress

What is unique about formation training is that it potentially encompasses the full range of physiologically induced stress responses. From a very slow, methodical building search to an active killing and everything else in between, your heart rate could fluctuate from a resting rate of 80 bpm to 220 bpm in a short span of time. We need to be aware of these physiological effects, construct our tactics accordingly, and learn strategies to manage them. Here are some things to consider.

Perception

Stress is related to how we interpret and react to events. Some events are stressful, but more so, it is how we perceive those events where the real stress occurs. People may react differently to the same situations. One person may interpret a situation as very stressful, while another person may not.

Training and building up confidence in your skills can change your perception of the threat in a given situation. Having a positive field experience is the king of confidence builders, so seek out those opportunities often and early to use and improve your skills. Perception is everything.

Commitment to Deadly Force

If you haven't already made a peace with yourself or your belief system with the taking of a human life, then not only might you hesitate when that critical moment arises, but you will be stressed during the time leading up to that event, exacerbating the stress of the situation itself. Do some soul-searching and come to a conviction or acceptance of this sooner rather than later, or else you will be a liability to yourself, your fellow officers, and the public. When you come to terms with the idea of taking a life and embrace the idea that it is a very real possibility, you will no longer fear it and your confidence will increase. With that increased confidence comes a reduction in stress, with that reduction in stress, better performance.

Maintaining Distance

Distance equals reaction time, and both are your allies. The more time you have, the better you can observe–orient–decide–act. What's referred to as the *reactionary gap,* is the distance between the officer and the subject required to safely formulate a reaction to an action. This distance or gap will vary, depending on the type of threat presented and the environment.

Regardless of the situation, this gap is your friend. We know that reaction is slower than action, and the research by the Force Science Institute can further your understanding of this. Furthermore, proximity of threat is a huge stress-enabling factor. Give yourself some distance.

Controlled or Tactical Breathing

We've already seen that an increased heart rate can enable other physiological responses to stress. Controlling your breathing reduces your heart rate and therefore can help manage your stress.

In times of stress, try inhaling through your nose for a count of four seconds, then hold your breath for four seconds, and then forcibly control the exhale over four seconds. Repeat this process for several cycles, at which time you should feel a reduction in your heart rate.

Try it right now for a full minute. Take your heart rate before and after, and compare the difference. This technique also works when you are having trouble falling asleep. If you practice controlled breathing regularly, you will find yourself doing it subconsciously. Now that's some next-level stuff.

Exercise

The human body uses several different energy systems. The most important for long-term, sustained energy is the aerobic system, which is developed through regular cardiovascular training. A well-known episode in the career of heavyweight boxer Muhammad Ali illustrates the value of a good aerobic system. In 1974, in about the fifth round of the heavyweight championship bout, Ali was getting mercilessly battered with body punches by a much larger and stronger champion, George Foreman. Describing this experience later in a television interview, Ali recalled a moment when he felt Foreman's punches were getting a little softer and thought to himself, *"Big George is getting tired."* He then concluded: *"This is the wrong place to get tired."* Ali waited for his stronger opponent to *punch himself out* and in round eight unloaded a flurry of punches that sent Foreman to the canvas for good.

On the street or in a combative encounter is also *the wrong place to get tired*. And it's preventable. Physically fit officers can cope with dramatic increases in heart rates due to stress or physical exertion more efficiently. Their heart rates stabilize and decrease faster, which aids in the reacquisition of fine and complex motor skills. Physical fitness also improves blood flow to the brain, bringing the additional sugars and oxygen that are needed when thinking intensely.

Being physically fit increases your confidence that you can stay in the fight and remain competent for as long as the situation requires, and thus reduces stress.

Mental Rehearsal

Mental rehearsal is the process of mentally visualizing and rehearsing how something should be done prior to physically doing it. This rehearsal connects thought processes with physical activity. Most of us are equipped with the physical tools (for example, defensive tactics or shooting skills) to get the job done, but if we don't connect them to a stimulus beforehand, a life-and-death decision process may happen too slowly or with errors. The point of mental rehearsal is to experience the situation before it occurs. Create real-life situations and walk through them, step by step and in as much detail as you can. If you've experienced similar events in training or in the field, your brain will treat this rehearsal as a virtual experience and neurons will start firing to create and reinforce those mental pathways, as if you're really experiencing the event. The scenario should be as real as possible and incorporate as much detail as you can manage, including sights, sounds, and smells. Then when you encounter a similar situation in real life, mentally it's as if you've been there before.

Most importantly, always visualize yourself winning and never, ever, give up.

Scanning

Earlier in the chapter I described certain visual issues resulting from stressful encounters. This is worth giving special attention to in our single formation training, because one of the system's keys to success is for officers to constantly adjust observance of their AORs. The greater their visual field, the greater success they'll have.

Scanning is the practice of breaking your tunnel vision by looking over each shoulder to forcefully override your brain's tendency to focus on one thing. Train for proper scanning by picking out specific things in the environment over your shoulders and behind you—a chair in the corner, for example—to avoid this becoming a frivolous head movement. In single-officer room entries, which are not preferred but sometimes unavoidable in the field, your peripheral vision becomes extremely important. Scanning is also essential during building searches and room clearings when taking a person into custody while there are still uncleared problem areas in a room.

Both scanning and tactical breathing can restore a huge range of your visual field.

Training

The importance of training goes without saying, and to discuss all the benefits of regular training would take over this book. Suffice it to say that skills are perishable, and regular and realistic training, such as that outlined in this primer, is essential to maintaining them. Positive training and field experiences will give you greater confidence in your abilities. Greater confidence reduces stress. A reduction in stress provides for optimal performance in the field.

Body Armour

Wearing body armour provides no guarantee of an officer's safety in a deadly force encounter, but it can help control stress levels because you know your survivability is enhanced while wearing it. Some of our training in room clearing will use a technique known as **squaring off** or **presenting armour**, which maximizes the life-saving potential of this important piece of personal protective equipment.

For more information on the effects of stress and ways to manage them, I highly recommend seeking out the research and training of PPCT, as this information has not been refuted in over three decades.

And finally, consider the following training principles that are well established in the fields of physiology and sports medicine. The following **Six General Principles** have been developed and proven for athletes by the National Strength and Conditioning Association in their text *Essentials of Strength Training and Conditioning*, but are also applicable to tactical training. I've paraphrased them for our purposes. Do your training programs adhere to these principles?

1. Individual Differences

The principle of **individual differences** means that because we all are unique individuals, we will each have a slightly different response to a training program. Every officer you train will have strengths and weaknesses. Your training style and the skills you are delivering, such as this tactical formation, need to accommodate individual differences and be user friendly for everyone, not just your rock-star students.

2. Overload

The scientific principle of **overload** states that a greater-than-normal stress or load on the body is required for training adaptation to take place. I apply this principle to skills training as well as to physical endurance. You need to recognize when your training repetitions are becoming stagnant and add new stimuli without overloading your students.

3. Progression

The principle of **progression** implies that there is an optimal level of overload that should be achieved, and an optimal timeframe within which this overload occurs. A gradual and systematic increase of the workload over a longer time will result in improvements in training (or skill) without risk of injury. If progression occurs too slowly, improvement is unlikely, but progression that is too rapid may result in negative training experiences.

4. Adaptation

Adaptation refers to the body's ability to adjust to increased or decreased physical demands. It is also one way we learn to coordinate muscle movement and develop specific skills, such as in formation training. Repeatedly practicing a skill or activity makes it second nature and easier to perform.

5. Use and Disuse

When it comes to training, you need to **use the skill or lose it**. When neurons fire together, they wire together: if they are not used, those cells will be recruited to be used somewhere else. Did you know that blind people have excellent hearing and an extremely developed visual cortex, even though they can't see? This is because the brain has recognized that cells that are of no use for vision can be recruited for the use of hearing and other senses. If not used regularly, your brain will put its resources to better use elsewhere. That's the way the brain works. Skills are perishable, so use them or lose them.

6. Specificity

The **specificity** principle simply states that training a certain body part or component of the body primarily develops that part. This implies that to become better at an exercise or skill, you must perform *that* exercise or skill. To learn how to fight, you fight. To improve your swimming, you swim. Our formation training needs to include repetitions ad nauseam, followed by positive field experiences.

Keeping these physiological effects of stress and management tools in mind as we move forward in our formation training and as you develop your programs will allow you to have realistic expectations of your officers and develop usable systems.

5

Basic Formations

> *A simple set of skills, combined with an emphasis on actions requiring complex and gross motor skills, all extensively rehearsed, allows for extraordinary performance levels under stress.*
>
> *Lt. Col. Dave Grossman; On Combat: The Psychology and Physiology of Deadly Conflict in War and in Peace*

This chapter demonstrates how a basic formation works and explains its components, using the model of officers conducting a slow, methodical building search that includes room entries.

When it comes to tactical formations, my mantra is *the simpler the better*. Complex systems may look far more impressive, but considering the training truths outlined in chapter 1—who we are training, how long we train, and how often our students will receive additional training after their initial instruction—it is unrealistic to expect our students to perform complex systems in the field, especially under stress. It is the simple system that can be retained over time against the erosion of disuse that will give officers success in the field.

As explained in the preface, the objective of this primer is to teach a single adaptable formation that can be used in the highest number of probable situations, ranging from a slow, methodical building search by uniformed patrol officers to the dynamic entry of a tactical unit to responding to an active killing in progress, such as a school shooting. For this reason I've omitted containment, breaching, and external movement techniques; discussion of room-clearing tactics will be general in nature.

I discourage readers from over-analyzing individual tactics presented in this chapter, since the purpose is to introduce a generic, widely used system and later show how students can be trained to adapt that formation effectively for different situations. If a diagram looks different than your experience suggests it should, I expect that, but don't get mired down in minor details and miss the bigger message.

Building Entry

The **file formation** is the most common formation and for good reason: it's extremely versatile. It is also known as the **column**, **stack**, or **line formation**. The team forms a column or "stacks up" at the point of entering a building and begins methodically clearing all areas as it moves through the environment. The number of members in the formation will vary, but we will begin with five, as shown in **Figure 5.1**.

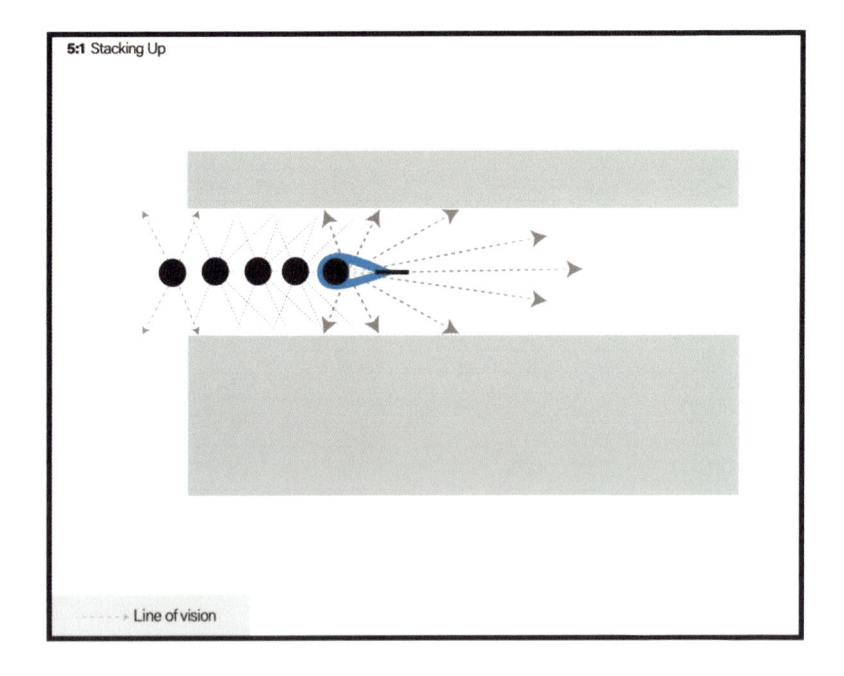

5:1 Stacking Up

Line of vision

The formation has a lead officer, who is the one making observations and decisions for the team, barring any other exigent circumstances. But remember that in the *Tactical Thinking Model*, every officer in the formation will have their own AOR (area of responsibility). The lead officer's AOR consists of everything in front of the team, but this will change frequently as the team conducts its search. The lead officer will decide which problem area needs to be addressed first.

Figure 5.2 shows the field of peripheral vision and, as illustrated, the potential for visual coverage is far-reaching. But let's not forget that stress has a huge physiological impact on our senses and abilities and loss of peripheral vision is one of those abilities affected.

5:3 Wall Gap

Wall Gap

83

Notice in **Figure 5.3** that the officers are not pressed directly against the wall. This is done intentionally because if shots are fired, bullets are more likely to travel along the wall than anywhere else. Best practice would have officers leave a gap between themselves and the wall.

The lead officer will announce the door she is staging on indicating the room she plans to enter and search. The verbal command in this case would be "door right." (see **Figure 3.1** *page 40*).

The officer behind will the *squeeze up* on the lead officer—which is just a grip on the shoulder or another designated area—nonverbally indicating to the lead officer that there is somebody with her. If she does not feel the squeeze up, then she will say, "Who's with me?" This will remind the trailing officer to squeeze up. But it also serves another purpose. It may confirm to the lead officer that there is no one with her and prompt her to post (stay in place). At this time, she will maintain a vigilant eye on her AOR/s, which in this diagram would be everything in front of her, and wait for additional resources.

As I've mentioned, the reason the officer does not turn around to communicate with her teammates is because to do so would be to take her eyes off her AOR. To do this for even for a moment would put herself and other officers at risk, since this gives the adversary a considerable advantage should a threat present itself in that moment. Officers must never neglect their AOR.

Static Threshold Evaluation

Once the lead officer knows a teammate is ready to enter the room with her, she will conduct a threshold evaluation. She may decide to cut the pie on the doorway, either statically or dynamically. For review, the purpose of cutting the pie is to locate the offender before he locates you. Cutting the pie on a doorway **statically** means to do so in a very slow and methodical fashion. If it's likely this won't enhance your ability to locate the offender before he locates you, then it's probably not a good tactical decision. Having said that, a slow and methodical threshold evaluation does have advantages. If a person is hiding in a closet or a room, for example, moving slowly around the threshold can allow officers to locate him first. Once the opponent is located, they can challenge him and follow the rule of thumb of **bringing the them to us**, or disengage and set up an armed and barricaded approach. These are probably the safest options.

Another big advantage of the slow threshold evaluation is that quite often, the challenge can be addressed without even penetrating the room.

For example if while cutting the pie, the officer observes a shoe or shoulder of the offender before the offender has located her, she has the enormous tactical advantage of ordering that person out of hiding and into the officer's environment without penetrating into the room. When officers penetrate the room, there is an increased risk the farther they penetrate. The prudent tactician will evaluate this. There are also negative factors to be considered.

Problems with Static Threshold Evaluation

It's commonly believed that moving in a slow and methodical fashion will always be the safest way to do things. However, there are times when moving more aggressively and decisively is better. Cutting the pie slowly may not be the best option when the room the officers are entering is in darkness and the hallway is lit up. This places the officer moving slowly and methodically across that threshold in an optimal kill zone for a person lying in wait in the darkness of the room.

Figure 5.4 shows how in this environment, the subject hiding in the room clearly holds the advantage, because the officer in the lit hallway can be clearly identified before she locates the subject. This is a breach of our tactical Thought Process and a textbook example of when not to statically cut the pie. In these instances, officers would be better off entering the room without hesitation and establishing a PRD (point of room domination) in the darkness, then begin using light to their tactical advantage.

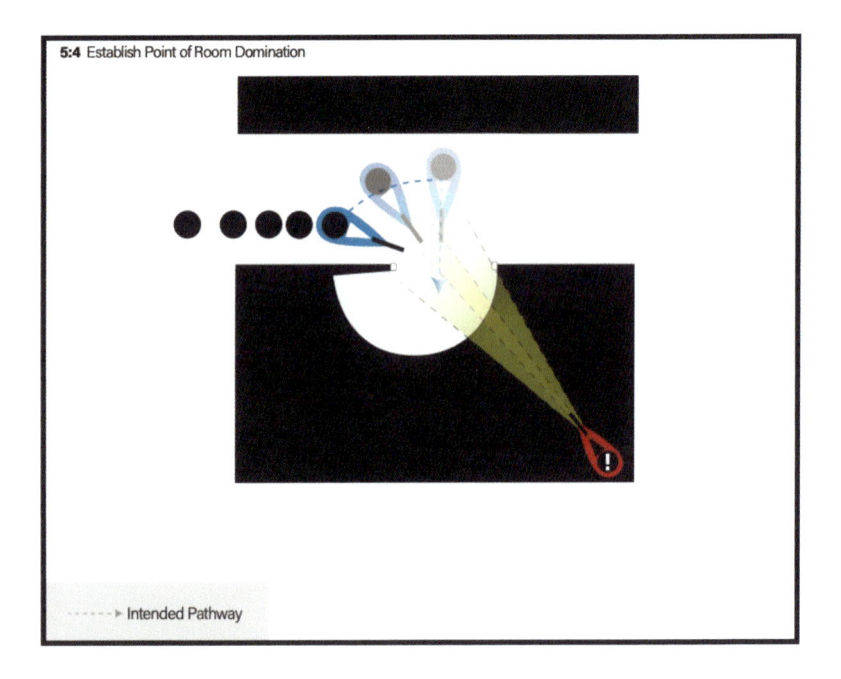

5:4 Establish Point of Room Domination

⋯▶ Intended Pathway

5:5 | 5:6 Unacceptable Thresholds

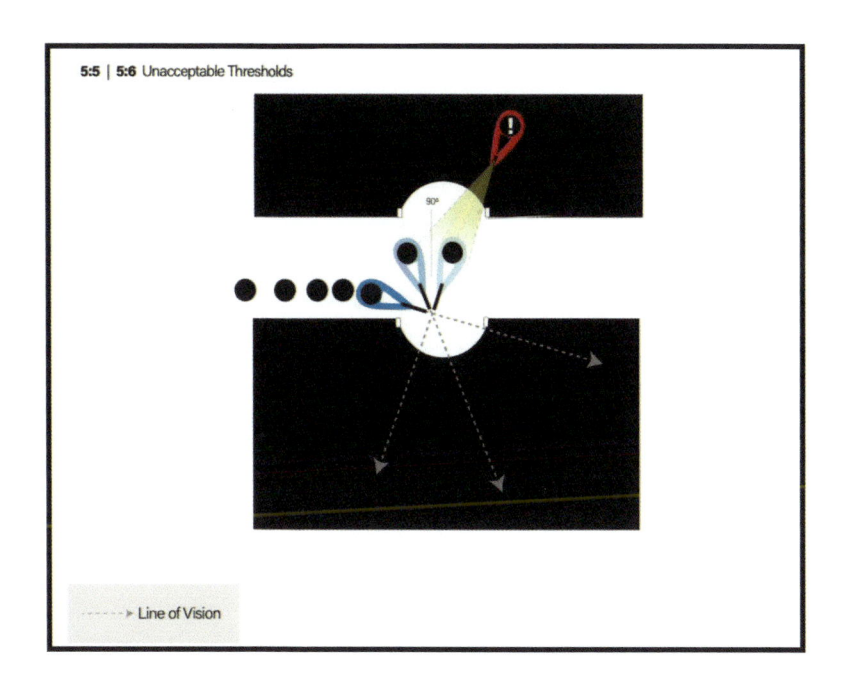

Line of Vision

Another time when cutting the pie slowly and methodically is not a good option is if it results in the officer turning her back to an uncleared problem area (**Figure 5.5**). There's incredible flexibility in this type of single formation, but some things should never be attempted except in exigent circumstances. **Unacceptable** is the term I use to refer to those situations or practices. Turning your back on uncleared problem areas is unacceptable.

As we move into the training component in the next chapter, I will demonstrate how situations like that illustrated in **Figure 5.5** are excellent opportunities to reinforce good decision-making and tactical thinking. It is the **brain we need to train,** and as trainers we must take advantage of instances like these to develop a tactical toolbox, if you will, and teach our students how to use those tools. We need to make good decision-makers out of our students as opposed to feeding them the answers to individual dilemmas.

Another *unacceptable* approach to a threshold evaluation is when an officer who is cutting the pie around a doorway violates the **90° rule** of firearms safety; that is, that the firearm's muzzle must never break a 45° angle to the left or the right of the line of fire (**Figure 5.6**). Firearms experts will tell you that this represents a danger to each officer should a gunfight erupt. For this same reason, as a general rule, *and with exception*, officers should not stage on either side of the doorway prior to

entering the room (**Figure 5.7**). If a threat emanates from the doorway, again this would pose a crossfire situation-unacceptable.

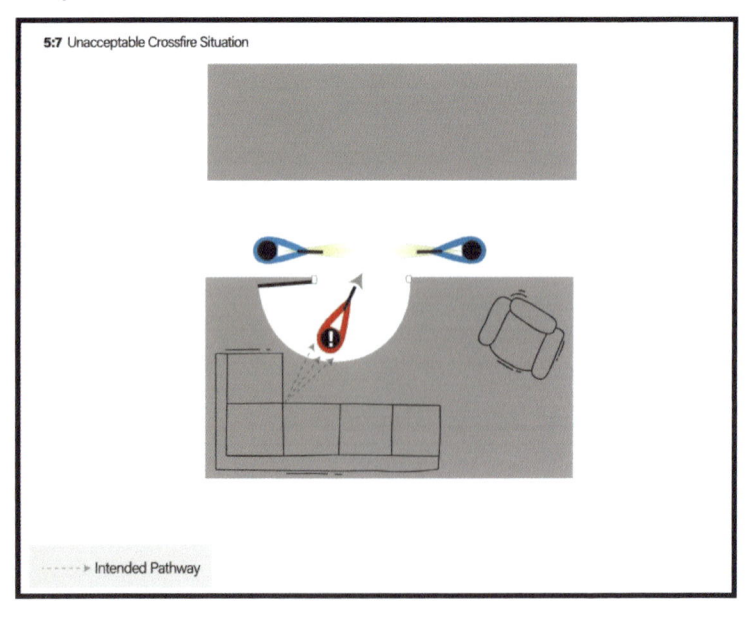

5:7 Unacceptable Crossfire Situation

Intended Pathway

88

Overly cautious threshold evaluations *sometimes* put officers at more risk than the safety they are intended to afford. If you've ever been fortunate enough to hear U.S. Army Lt. Col. (ret.) Dave Grossman speak, you may have heard his story about walking in the dark wooded area of his property with his grandson. As the day grew later and darker, Grossman's grandson became nervous and thought that they should get back to the house. When Grossman asked why, his grandson replied something to this effect: *"Because it's dark."* Grossman answered: *" What's wrong with the dark? Darkness is your friend."* The child was scared because *"there's bad things in the dark."* Grossman kneeled, put a hand on his grandson's shoulder, looked him straight in the eye and replied: *"Yeah. It's us."* I love that story because it illustrates a hunting mind-set and so succinctly reflects the attitude we need to adopt in order to be successful in critical encounters.

Things sometimes get scary and we do need to exercise great caution. Please don't misunderstand me: if scuffling is heard inside a room confirming a presence, or the assistance of a police service dog indicates a suspect inside a room, or there is reliable information that the person inside has a firearm, I am not suggesting officers should plow aggressively into that room, unless of course there's an imminent threat to life. That would just be reckless, and if that were the situation, we would draw upon one of our rules of thumb and **bring the suspect to us**. Options for dealing with this might be issuing challenges, deploying chemicals, K-9, or cameras and other technology, to name a few—my point is that there is sometimes an advantage to moving with confidence and decisiveness, overwhelming the assailant, and removing his time to think. We are trained, we have the weapons and the assistance to respond better than anyone.

We need to adopt a *hunter's* mindset. If anyone needs to be afraid, it's the offender.

Dynamic Threshold Evaluation

This form of threshold evaluation holds advantages that come from initiative and aggression. One way to interfere with the offender's thought process is to limit their time to think. The slow and methodical way of cutting the pie is sometimes appropriate but at other times it's better to move **fluidly**. This is not to be confused with rushing; moving at a brisk walk or as fast as you can accurately shoot are commonly believed to be the optimal speed to move, but more so, you should never move so fast that you can't accurately process the information you're receiving. The reason, at times, it may be better to enter a room **fluidly** is because often the hallway is the most dangerous place to be. Spending an unnecessary amount of time evaluating a threshold or stalling in the hallway may leave officers in a potential kill zone for too long.

One thing that is often forgotten is that cutting the pie on the doorway and evaluating that threshold already begins when an officer is approaching the doorway (**Figure 5.8**). As the officer moves toward the point of room entry, he has already begun to observe what's in the room. Even though the lead officer's AOR includes the hallway, he is also taking in information about the next door he's going to go through. It's impossible not to have these observations, and critical to **deal with the real threat before the perceived threat**.

5:8 Dynamic Threshold

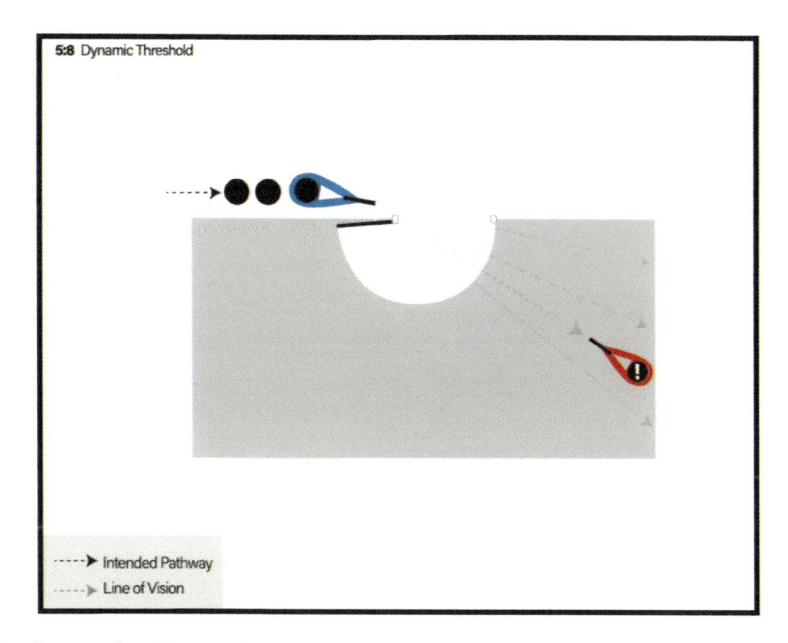

→ Intended Pathway
→ Line of Vision

To dynamically evaluate a threshold on a doorway is not to omit cutting the pie, it's simply to do it more aggressively and fluidly, without stalling or hesitating.

Room Entry

Once the lead officer has made his threshold evaluation, announced the door, and received his squeeze up, he enters the room. On doing so, he will *square off* in the doorway (**Figure 5.9**).

Squaring off in the doorway is the practice of "presenting" your weapons and body armour for maximum effectiveness and response options. If the officer turns to his side, for example, that is not the optimal position for his body armour to take gunfire because there are separations in the soft body armour. Nor is it the optimal position from which to return fire if fired upon. Body armour is meant to take gunfire head-on, so that's how an officer should present it. In addition, firearms readiness means having eliminated one more thing to do, such as drawing the firearm and pointing it in the right direction to respond to the threat.

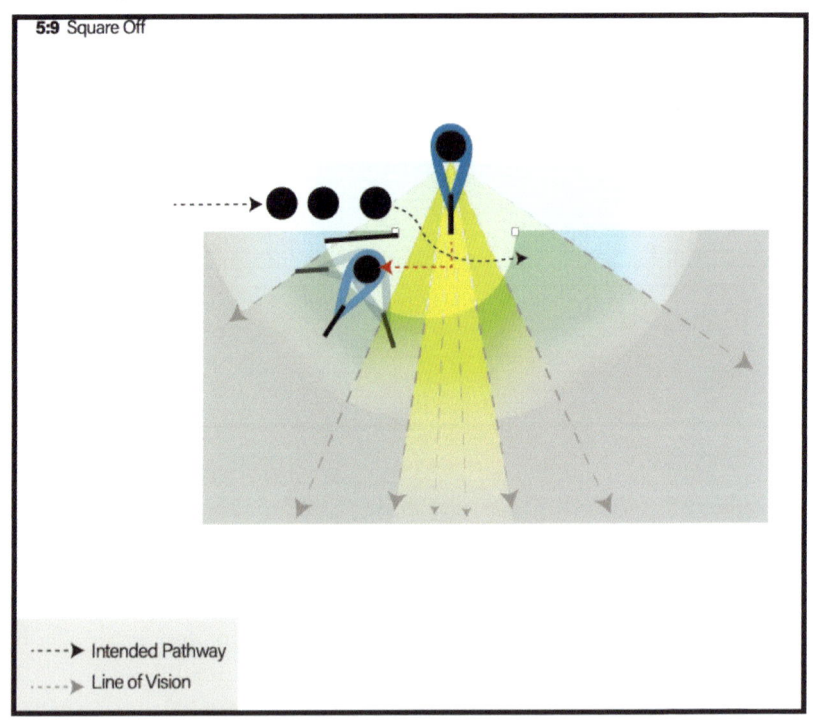

5:9 Square Off

·····▶ Intended Pathway
·····▶ Line of Vision

This is an excellent example of how to improve our thought process, by enhancing our ability to **react** to a threat and hindering the offender's ability to **attack** us successfully. Furthermore, squaring off at the point of entry allows the entering officer to get a visual snapshot of the room. This snapshot enables the officer to **assess** and evaluate his options prior to entering the room. If the officer has contact with a person who is perceived to be a threat, he may be able to engage that threat from outside the threshold of the room. In addition to giving the officer the option to engage, squaring off on the doorway also gives him the option of disengaging and using the doorway to his tactical advantage. (To be clear, an officer should never remain static in the doorway. **Figure 5.9** is meant to show the practice of squaring off, not suggesting the officer stops moving while doing so.)

By curling around a doorway *without* squaring off, not only is the officer denying himself a quick snapshot view of the room prior to entering, he's also putting himself at a considerable physical disadvantage.

Point of Room Domination (PRD)

Once inside the room, the lead officer can either go straight or button hook. The decision does not have to be predetermined with his partner, as the partner already knows that she will be reading off the lead officer's movement. What the lead officer decides to do next depends a lot on what he has learned during the threshold evaluation. He will want to face the unknown area as soon as possible. If during the threshold evaluation he observes a wall running along the doorway, such as with a corner-feeding room (as in **Figure 5.11**), he may reasonably decide the threat is less likely to emanate from that area. Or if during the approach he has had the opportunity to observe the area directly ahead of him, as the first officer in the door he should first go to the area from which a threat is most likely to emanate.

Once inside the room, team members establish a PRD just inside the entranceway (**Figure 5.10**). They will ensure they have moved completely out of the entranceway, when practical, in order to hinder the subject's ability to locate them. The PRD can assume different shapes and will not always afford the officers full doorway clearance, as illustrated in **Figure 5.11**, where the room entrance is corner feeding.

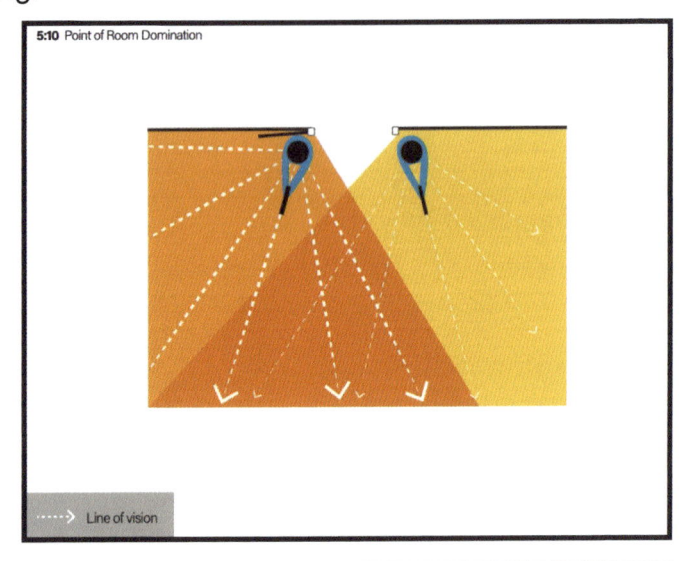

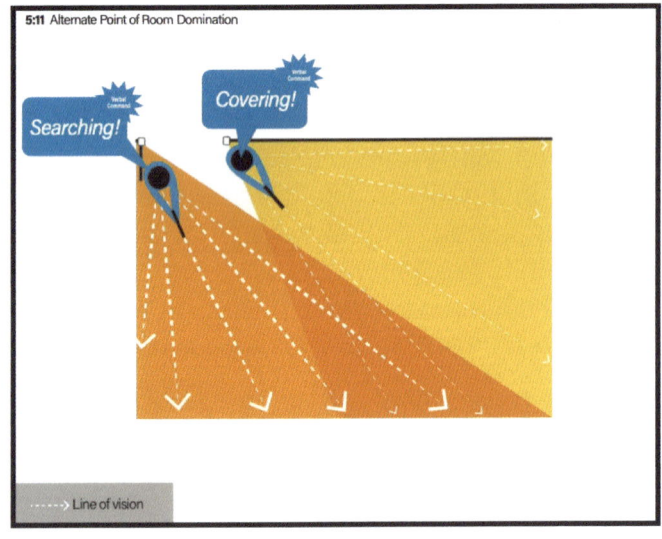

5:10 Point of Room Domination

·····> Line of vision

5:11 Alternate Point of Room Domination

Searching!

Covering!

·····> Line of vision

The benefit of the PRD is that the officers can engage the subject, and often visually clear most if not all of the room from that point. But in addition, occupying the PRD affords officers the critical ability to disengage and get out of the room if that's their best option. Tactical thinking becomes crucial at this stage, as each officer will identify their AOR.

Once the PRD is established, officers designate themselves as either a covering or a searching officer and make that verbal announcement. These roles are subject to change if an officer recognizes that her problem area should be cleared first, in which case she simply switches roles with her partner (**Figure 5.12**). You cannot search without cover, so it is the covering officer who should make the first announcement.

When officers are executing this part of an entry, there is a tendency to get caught up in the flow of the team movement and be hasty. Once officers establish their PRD, it is time to take a breath, slow things down, evaluate the room and the work that needs to be done,

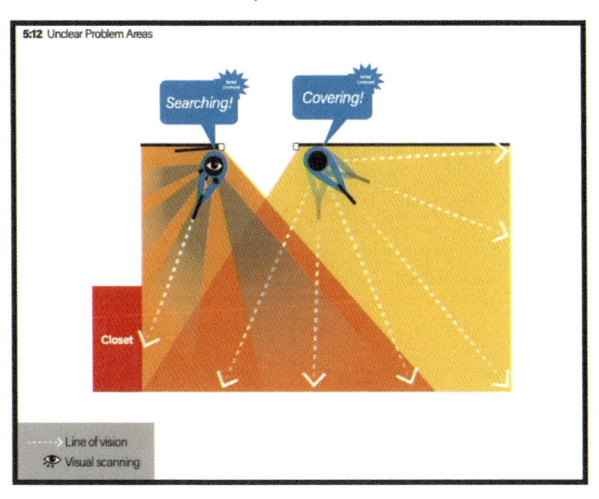

5:12 Unclear Problem Areas

and communicate with partners how they are going to do it. Room-clearing tactics are both abundant and debatable, so as indicated earlier, I will not delve into the minutiae of clearing each room or area. To address this topic effectively would require an entire chapter (if not its own book) and take our discussion away from the single formation theory. However, as a standard operating procedure, the Thought Process becomes your best friend when covering and searching uncleared problem areas. When deciding which tactic would be best, ask the simple question: *"Will this tactic allow me to locate, react to, identify, and/or control the opponent before he can locate, react, and attack me?"*

Contact

If officers have contact—that is, they encounter a suspect—proper tactical thinking will dictate that this become their focal point and take the highest priority. It is not necessary for officers to announce "contact," because once they start issuing loud verbal commands, that will signify to other members of the team that contact has been made.

Officers should obey our rules of thumb and **give the real threat priority over the perceived threat** and **bring the subject to us** whenever that is possible, rather than penetrate further than is absolutely needed into the uncleared problem area.

Officers will take the suspect into custody according to their organization's policy and how they were trained. If they feel that they can do that safely with two officers, they will do so. If additional officers are required, this is when the verbal command "trailers" is used to announce that backup is needed.

There is always debate on whether the room should be cleared before restraining the suspect, or vice versa. Which comes first depends on both the environment and the suspect's behaviour. If the suspect is compliant and officers can clear a small area without putting themselves in a position of disadvantage by turning their backs to uncleared problem areas while restraining the suspect, doing that first is a good option.

If a suspect's compliance appears to have an expiry date and officers feel an urgency to restrain him as soon as possible, they should do so. But again, while turning one's back to uncleared problem areas is sometimes unavoidable, such as in a violent encounter, it should be avoided whenever possible (revisit **Figure 2.7**).

Once the officers have cleared their areas, they will announce "clear" and proceed out of the area to rejoin the team and continue the search. To avoid any confusion, officers will announce "coming out" so they don't startle other officers in the hall (**Figure 5.13**).

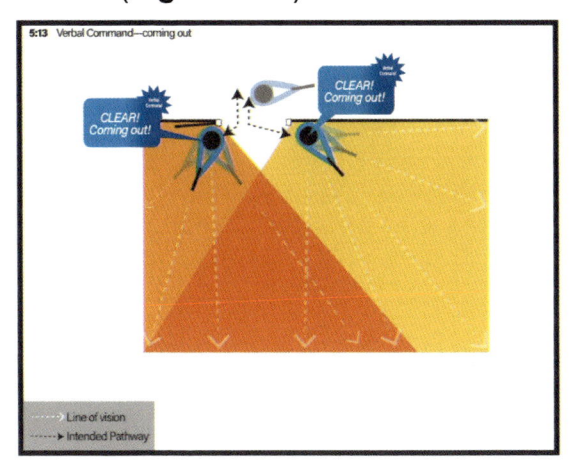

97

There should always be at least one officer in the open area where other officers will rejoin the team after clearing their AORs. This should be considered when officers are staging at doorways and entering rooms. If the common area (such as a hallway) is left unoccupied when officers evaluate a threshold and enter that room, that is unacceptable. What should happen instead is that one or more officers stand by until there are sufficient resources to carry on, as illustrated by the fifth officer in **Figure 5.14**. If the hallway or common area is left unoccupied, officers emerging from rooms that they have cleared will have no frame of reference for what has been cleared and what has not. At best, this raises the possibility of having to determine what work has been done or redoing it. At worst, it creates the significant risk of officers moving past areas that have not been cleared. For these reasons, it is necessary to assign a single supervisor or team leader to serve as a semi-objective overseer to avoid these issues. When officers emerge from clearing their areas, they can seek out the supervisor and announce "looking for work," or just observe where their team members are and rejoin them.

As a beneficial exercise, I recommend that everyone involved in training role-play as the suspect at some point and lie in wait, with the mind-set of wanting to hurt or kill the officer. Listen for the sounds and watch for the sights that allow you to **locate** and **attack** the officer. Follow this and other drills with the honest, ego-free conversations that will enhance your abilities to be better in the field, when these kind of situations are real.

Using one room as an example, this chapter has described the basic building search process. **Figure 5.14** is worth studying, as it illustrates how the search would continue and progress though the rest of this environment. Aside from small changes, most searches and entries are conducted in this fashion. Consider this a frame of reference as we move forward and begin to explore how to adapt our formations to changing environments and situations.

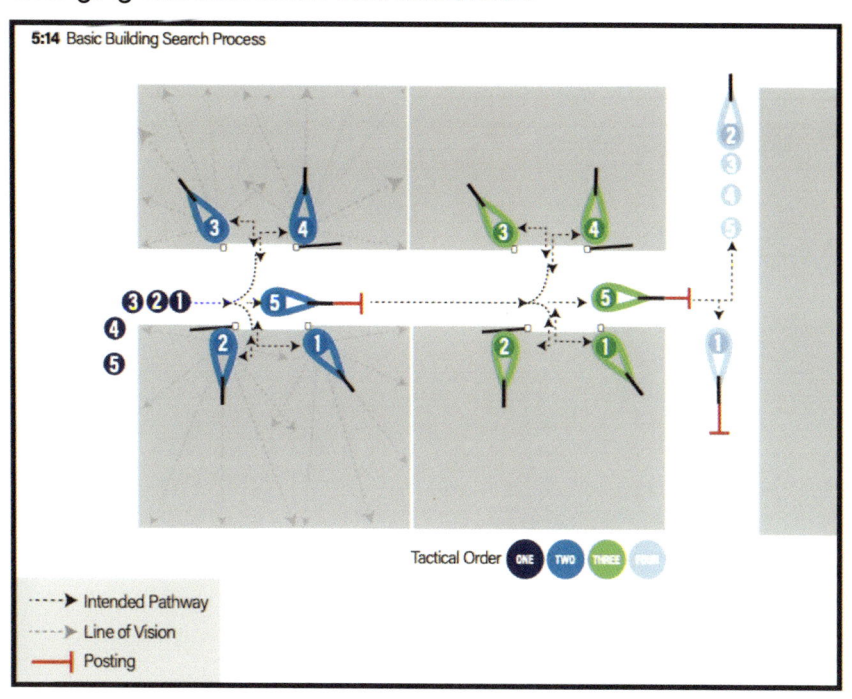

5:14 Basic Building Search Process

- - -▶ Intended Pathway
- - -▶ Line of Vision
———| Posting

This is the essence and beauty of authentic, principle-based training. In view of the realities, limitations, and factors I have discussed, attempting to develop individual tactics for each situation would be to train officers for failure. But if officers are well versed in key principles and tactical thought processes, they will make the best possible decisions for the highest-probability challenges. Let these tactical thinking principles be the answer key to resolving specific dilemmas.

6

Training the Brain

*Tell me and I forget.
Teach me and I may remember.
Involve me and I learn.*

Benjamin Franklin

Formation training should begin with the most basic, low-stress building search and slowly progress from there. Now that we've had a good look at a basic formation, it will much easier to conceptualize a more flexible version of the same thing. For this to be successful, all members of the formation need to have a thorough understanding of *what they are doing and why they are doing it.*

The principles discussed earlier in the book—the Thought Process, the OODA Loop, the Tactical Thinking Model, as well as the rules of thumb and modes of verbal and non-verbal communication—all play a vital role. In order for students to internalize these principles, trainers need to include many repetitions of training drills. Whenever a student asks me how many repetitions are enough, my answer is always the same: *more*. If you want your training to be sound, you cannot do too many repetitions. Training may get a little rote or boring, your students may roll their eyes, but in stressful environments those skills will be available to them and they will thank you later.

With the challenge as complex as developing a formation suitable for everything from a tactical building search to a mass murder in progress in unknown and varying environments, it *is* possible, and even common, to develop a different solution or formation to effectively respond to each of them and have them meet a standard by the end of the training day.

However, developing a single formation adaptable for the highest probabilities—as opposed to every possibility—is the most realistic approach. The best thing we can do for our people is to train so exhaustively in the basics, with such an emphasis on the operating principles that when the unforeseen and unrehearsed challenges present themselves in the field, and they will, our officers will respond in a tactically sound manner.

How do we do this?

Basic formation training such as the type discussed in the previous chapter can and should be done rudimentarily and with little discussion. However, with more advanced training, I've found incredible success in conducting something I call a *Socratic instructional discussion* between teacher and student before each exercise. Through this, the teacher encourages the students to verbalize their understanding of the underlying principles and thought process they should be applying; the student basically describes what they are planning to do and the reason they are doing it. I'll demonstrate this shortly. This kind of teaching and instructional discussion should take up approximately 10% to 20% of your training time, and working on the physical drills (to reinforce subconscious learning), the remaining 80% to 90% of the time. When training officers, each component, for example the threshold evaluation with the room entry, should be taught and exercised in independent evolutions, so that when the more complex team movement begins, the students are proficient at each skill or component, and then it is built upon.

In other words, teach your officers one element at a time and make sure they are competent in that before moving on to the next technique. This is what I referred to in chapter 4 as the principle of **progression**. Furthermore, by isolating one skill set you eliminate all other distracting elements to ensure a complete focus on that one skill.

I personally like to begin with training in pairs, two officers conducting a threshold evaluation. To isolate the subject matter, I instruct the students to only identify the door they plan to enter, announce that door, squeeze up, read off, slowly cut the pie on the doorway, enter the room while squaring off on the doorway, establish a PRD (point of room domination), announce "covering" and "searching," and stop there. This is more than enough for beginners to start with, and skilled operators as a refresher, and as you will see, there will be plenty of teaching points along the way. I recommend eliminating any additional stimuli such as searching and clearing the room, or managing multiple AORs (areas of responsibility) such as other rooms down the hallway at the beginning.

Isolate—master—progress—repeat.

The sequence of drills should be broken down this way, so as not to *overload* students. This might sound overly simple, but there are many benefits to compartmentalizing these skills. Overall, this process builds a greater understanding, confidence and competence. If you build a house with a faulty foundation, the entire structure is unstable. Skill sets need to be built on a sturdy foundation, one solid brick at a time.

A typical training outline might look something like the following:

Drill	Technique	Time
1	- 2-officer room entry, open doors only - address corners and scan room - read-off principle - establish PRD, ensure safe weapons handling (90° rule) - no search, no hallway AORs - STATIC CUTTING THE PIE - bio feedback for cutting the pie ("bad guy" role player)	1 hour
2	- Everything above, now incorporate closed doors, small rooms, etc., as instructor sees fit	1 hour
3	- 2-officer room entry, all rooms - establish PRD - announce "covering" and "searching" - clear rooms - FLUIDLY CUTTING THE PIE	1 hour
4	- introduce adversary (compliant) in random rooms - announce "contact," clear room, complete handcuffing - begin experimenting with lights (on in room, off in hallway; vice versa)	1 hour
5	- 4 to 6 team movement, room entry and clearing - introduce covering uncleared AORs - "posting," "blue on blue," stairwells, locked doors, etc.	Reminder of day (4 hrs.)

An outline like this allows students to learn one component at a time before moving on. A word of caution though, when the students move on to the next evolution, the tendency is to neglect the proficiencies achieved in the previous evolution. This needs to be recognized and discouraged.

With each of these drills, the reasons for using certain tactics and what their underlying principles are should be reviewed during the instructional discussion. For example, if a student decides to slowly and methodically cut the pie on a closet space during a room-clearing drill, the instructor should encourage the independent thinking but openly explore the reasoning behind it. The correct reasoning is that she feels it would be the best way to **locate** the suspect before the suspect can **locate** the officer, in agreement with the Thought Process. Once the instructor has received this answer, the student can proceed, with praise and encouragement for her sound tactical decision making. By conducting your training in this way, you encourage desirable behaviour and empower students to make independent decisions while reinforcing basic principles in the back of their minds. Conversely, if the student is cutting the pie on a doorway and it doesn't afford the advantage of locating the suspect first, this should be corrected and explained, thus decreasing the frequency of ineffective choices. This is basic, classical conditioning that behavioural psychologist B.F. Skinner would approve of.

This discussion process requires a lot of patience in the beginning, but remember that tactical training doesn't come as easily for some people as for others, and we all need to start somewhere. Patience and nurturing are the key to building confident and capable students.

Once each training evolution is completed, another layer of the onion is added progressively. Again, this is a whole new type of thinking and experience for most students, so patience is a virtue. Remember that **training the brain** is our mission.

Instructional Discussions

Before each drill, the instructor addresses every student in turn in an instructional discussion. The first student is asked specific questions to ensure he's utilizing a principle-based approach to problem solving and thinking properly (**Figure 6.1**). The dialog might go something like this:

Instructor: What is your area of responsibility?

Student 1: Everything in front of me.

Instructor: What are you going to do first?

Student 1: I'm going to clear this room on my right.

Instructor: How are you going to evaluate the threshold?

Student 1: I'm going to cut the pie, but fluidly. as opposed to statically.

Instructor: Why?

Student 1: To locate the bad guy before he can locate me, like in the Tactical Thought Process.

Instructor: Why cut the pie fluidly instead of statically?

Student 1: Because in this case, the light is on in the hallway and not in the room. Moving slowly would defeat the purpose of cutting the pie. I'd rather just square off on the doorway, get in the room, and establish the point of room domination.

Instructor: Outstanding! Are you going in by yourself?

Student 1: Oh yeah! I'll announce "door right" and wait for the squeeze up.

Instructor: And if you don't get the squeeze up?

Student 1: I'll say, "Who's with me?"

In case you haven't noticed, this is an exceptional student. Not all instructional discussions go so smoothly, but this gives an idea of the type of conversation that needs to happen to get students thinking independently about what they are doing and why they are doing it. It also makes them accountable for their decisions. Most importantly, the instructional discussion *involves* the students in their learning and keeps them engaged, as opposed to listening to the instructor ramble on and on.

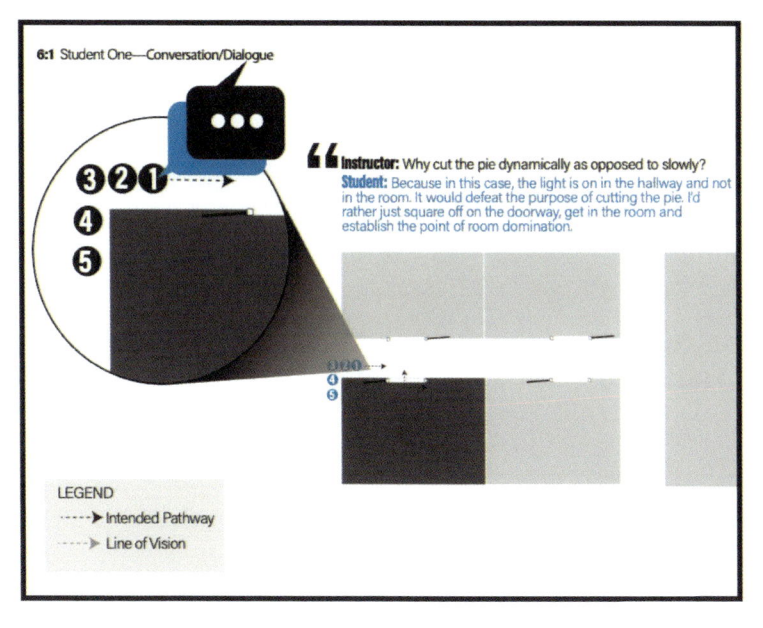

6:1 Student One—Conversation/Dialogue

> **Instructor:** Why cut the pie dynamically as opposed to slowly?
> **Student:** Because in this case, the light is on in the hallway and not in the room. It would defeat the purpose of cutting the pie. I'd rather just square off on the doorway, get in the room and establish the point of room domination.

LEGEND
----▶ Intended Pathway
----▶ Line of Vision

6:2 Student Two—Conversation/Dialogue

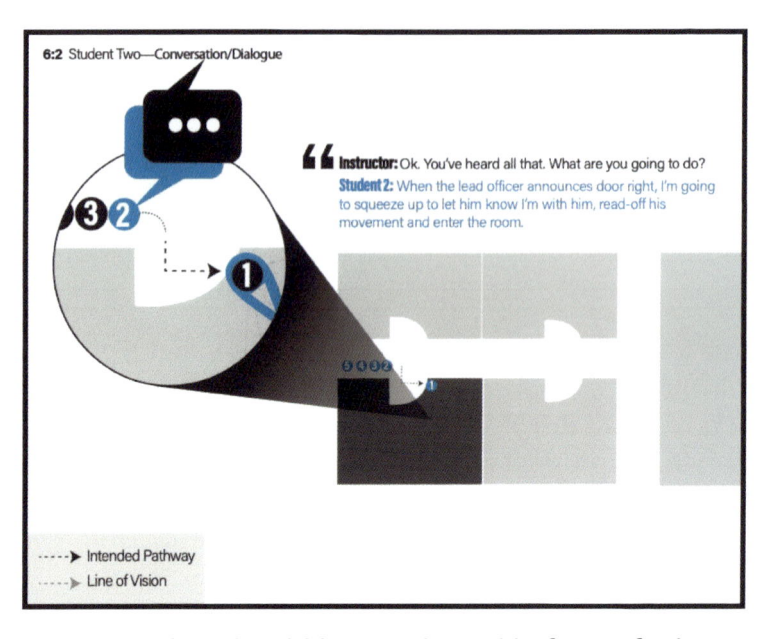

Instructor: Ok. You've heard all that. What are you going to do?
Student 2: When the lead officer announces door right, I'm going to squeeze up to let him know I'm with him, read-off his movement and enter the room.

- - -▶ Intended Pathway
- - -▶ Line of Vision

All this discussion should be conducted in front of other students to encourage observational learning as well. By doing this, everyone benefits from each other's learning, resulting in an enhanced and expedited experience for students and teacher. Furthermore, this discussion should be taken right down the formation line before allowing anyone to proceed. The instructional discussion with the second member of the formation (**Figure 6.2**) would go something like this:

Instructor: OK. You've heard all that. What are you going to do?

Student 2: When the lead officer announces "door right," I'm going to squeeze up to let him know I'm with him.

Instructor: What's your area of responsibility?

Student 2: Primarily to read off the officer in front of me, but I'll also watch down the hall or other uncleared problem areas.

Instructor: What happens if the officer in front of you makes a mistake and passes an uncleared problem area to go into another door?

Student 2: I would still read off his movement and stay with him, using the read off to self-correct. It would be the responsibility of the officer behind me to also recognize the error and correct it by proceeding with her trailing member to that uncleared area.

Wow, this class is good! The conversation then moves to the third team member and proceeds in a similar fashion throughout the entire formation. The group is then allowed to proceed through the motions that they just described, and no further. Once that drill is done, the process begins again with a fresh discussion. Be patient, because students learning via this method will acquire the right tactical thinking and internalize the key principles extremely quickly—before long, you will have to slow them down.

The training environment should be kept relatively simple and static until the students have demonstrated that they are confident and competent with the principles and tactics. More challenging tasks may be added incrementally at a rate that allows students to work through them, yet is not overwhelming. Depending on your training environment, these challenges may present themselves organically, or you may need to manufacture them.

Figure 6.3 illustrates such a challenge where two doorways are opposite each other. This is where the instructional discussion should begin again, allowing students to exercise their newfound tactically sound and principle-based thought process.

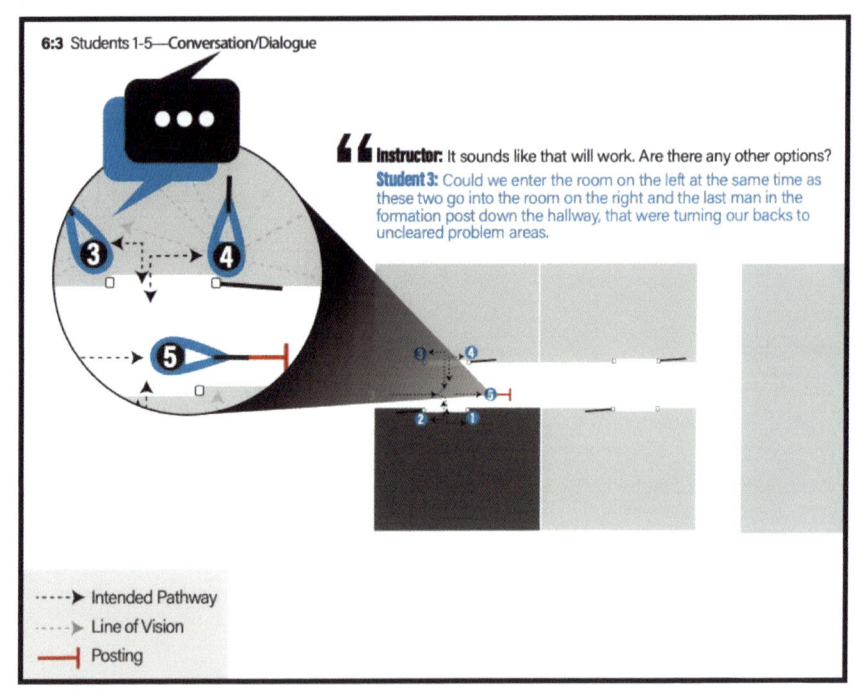

6:3 Students 1-5—Conversation/Dialogue

Instructor: It sounds like that will work. Are there any other options?

Student 3: Could we enter the room on the left at the same time as these two go into the room on the right and the last man in the formation post down the hallway, that were turning our backs to uncleared problem areas.

- Intended Pathway
- Line of Vision
- Posting

At this point in the training, some instructors may feel tempted to feed the answers to students, or maybe even consider changing to a different formation for that unique situation. This is tempting, but it is exactly the wrong thing to do. The right thing here is to allow the students to work through the problem with the basics and principles they've already begun to internalize. In this case, the next instructional discussion might go something like this:

Instructor: How are you going to manage this?

Student 1: I'm going to go into the room on my right, announce "door right," and move into the room.

Student 2: I'm going to squeeze up on the lead and read off her movement, so proceed into the room on the right and clear that room with her.

Student 3: I'm going to post on the hallway until they are done clearing that room.

Student 4: I guess then I could post on the uncleared room on the left.

Instructor: It sounds like that will work. Are there any other options?

Student 3: Could we enter the room on the left at the same time as these two go into the room on the right, and the last one in the formation post down the hallway so that we're not turning our backs to uncleared problem areas?

Can they?

Yes, they can! Neither option is wrong. As a matter of fact, this is the critical tactical thinking you've been looking for as a trainer, and it is a joyous moment to see it take hold. If the students are adhering to the principles they've been taught and avoiding *unacceptable* practices, such as turning their backs to uncleared problem areas, there is nothing wrong with either solution. What's more, you've begun to instil a tactically sound manner of thinking so that when problems emerge in the field, your people can adjust on the fly and then move on. You don't need a new formation, you just need one with the flexibility to adapt to new challenges but without losing the communicative adhesives that bind the formation—such as reading off, squeezing up, and the verbal commands.

In addition, remember the advantages of aggressive action. Spending an unnecessary amount of time in a hallway—a potential kill zone, being overly cautious, or attempting to construct a complex entry strategy can be more dangerous than the safety it is intended to ensure. In some instances, inside the room is a safer place to be. I will qualify this by re-emphasizing that if we believe that an adversary is in a room, armed and waiting, unless there is an imminent threat to life we should contain that threat and use our resources to manage that situation, such as a employing a tactical unit with cameras, imaging equipment, and superior weapons, or calling in a police K-9 unit, to name a few options. At times like these we need to slow everything down. But there *are* circumstances when acting decisively and with authority not only removes the opponent's time to think and formulate a plan, it can also be extremely psychologically intimidating and foster compliance on its own. These things must be considered.

Another consideration is that by issuing verbal commands you may be compromising your position and enhancing the suspect's ability to locate you. This contradicts the Tactical Thought Process. Some people may opt for hand signals to avoid this problem. My goal is simplicity, and for that reason I don't use hand signals. It is also my experience that when a group of individuals trains together enough, verbal commands become very economical and are sometimes not even required. For example, in the middle of a smoothly flowing entry or search by an experienced group, when the officer in front stages at a doorway, it can be understood through the vastly underrated non-verbal communicators and body language, that she is going into the room on her right. The officer behind her can automatically squeeze up and the officers will enter the room together. This intuitive communication comes after a lot of experience and training. However, as a best practice, communication should never be compromised, especially with less experienced students.

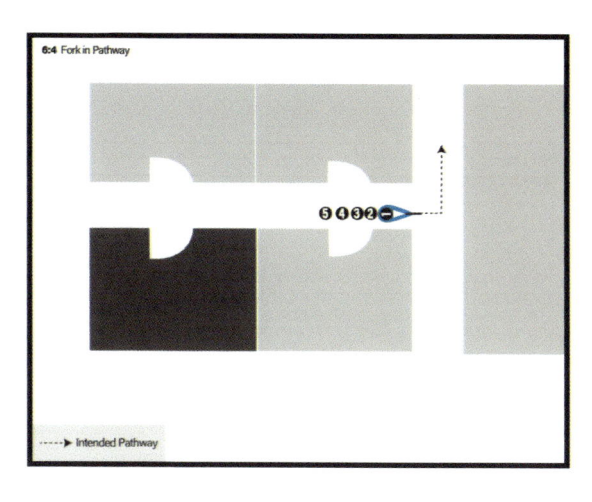

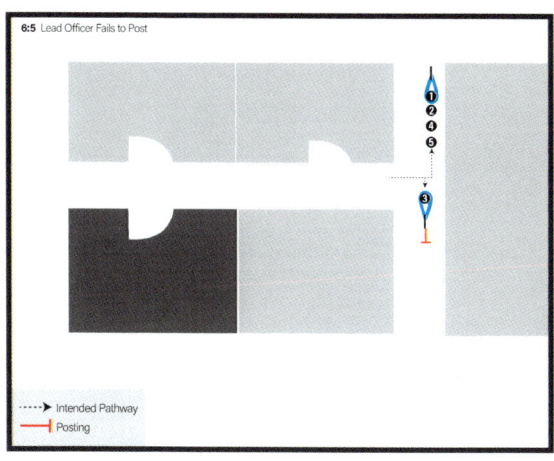

6:4 Fork in Pathway

·····▶ Intended Pathway

6:5 Lead Officer Fails to Post

·····▶ Intended Pathway
—| Posting

As team members move through this environment they come to a fork, a choice of two hallways in which to proceed (**Figure 6.4**). Again, the same *Socratic Instructional Discussion* should take place. At this point, the appropriate choice is for the lead officer to post on one hallway while the rest of the officers move down the other hallway and continue clearing in the same fashion.

If the lead officer fails to post (**Figure 6.5**), this is not a show stopper; the show must go on. The second officer should read off the officer in front of him and follow him down the hall. The third officer should realize that nobody has posted on the opposite hall and fill that role. Errors happen all the time, even among experienced officers and teams. This is precisely why the read off is so critical, as it is the ultimate self-correcting tool. To the casual observer, this mistake would not even be noticed.

Likewise, if the second officer decides to post, the third officer should seamlessly fall in behind the lead officer as they proceed down the hallway. With more training, these actions become smoother. With more practice and repetition, your officers will immediately notice the holes or AORs not being covered. This is the essence of good tactics: **covering off all areas and filling in the gaps.**

Now, what happens if the environment changes; for example, if the team encounters a large area such as a gymnasium or the hallway widens? (**Figure 6.6**).

Again, the starting point is an instructional discussion in which students are gently nudged to adjust their positions and adapt to the new environment so as to enhance their coverage of their AORs while adhering to the principles.

6:6 Amoeba vs Straight Formation

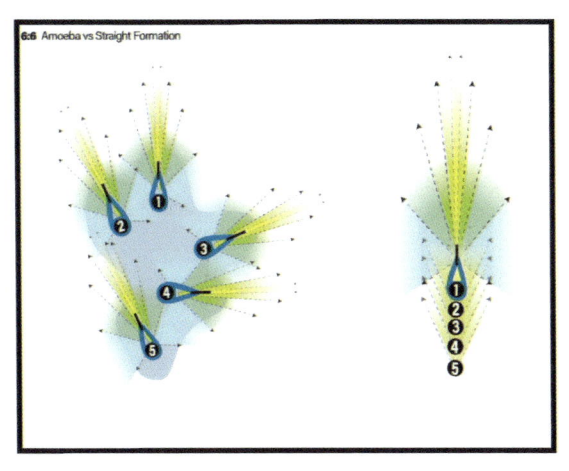

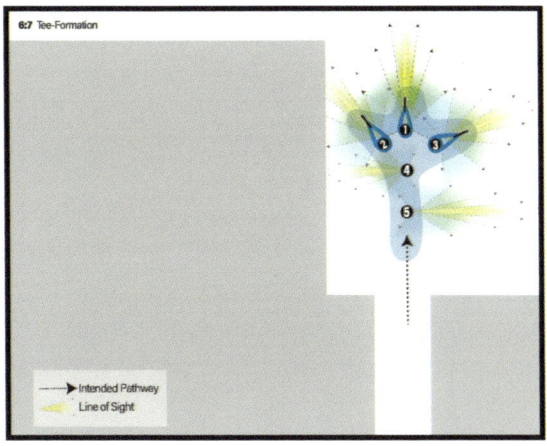

6:7 Tee-Formation

➤ Intended Pathway
Line of Sight

This is where the amoeba formation really starts to take its shape, or lack thereof. Each officer is thinking in a principle-based and tactically sound manner—that is, they are self-questioning their positions and making decisions that will enhance their vantage point or expand coverage of their AORs as well as shortening their thought process (locate, react, assess, or control).

In **Figure 6.7**, the lead officer's position hasn't changed but the second officer has figured out that because he was tucked in behind the lead officer, his field of vision was compromised and his pistol positioning, although pointed in a safe direction, was not optimal, compromising his ability to react to an emanating threat. He thinks his position could be more optimal if he fans out slightly from the rigidity of the column formation to his left. The third officer follows suit to the right, and the fourth and fifth officers make minor adjustments.

As you can see by the graphic representation of visual fields, a few alert members of the formation have greatly enhanced its effectiveness. To the untrained eye, it may look like a sloppy Tee formation, but what is not compromised by the tactically informed members of this *amoebic f*ormation is the read off. In a Tee formation, it is unclear who the lead officer is, and thus who the other officers will read off. Nor does the Tee formation have the flexibility to compress and expand with the changing environment. Furthermore, the Tee formation is more rigid, thus less conducive to linking up with other officers; and finally, it's a different formation for officers to learn, which presents a challenge given the usual time limitations for training.

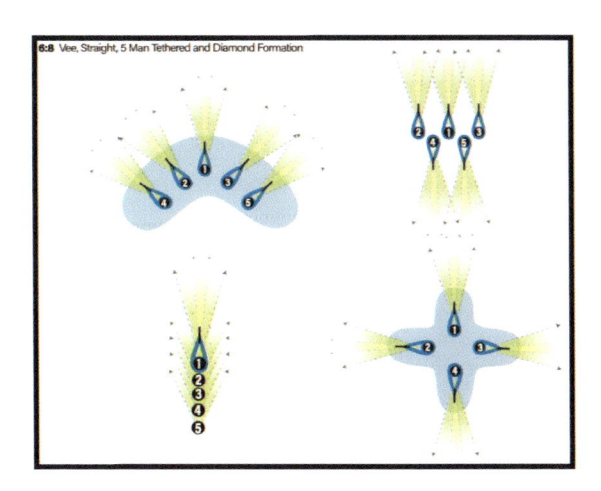

6:8 Vee, Straight, 5 Man Tethered and Diamond Formation

The same points can be made, in varying degrees, with respect to other formations such as the Vee or diamond formations (**Figure 6.8**). All these formations have their strengths and weaknesses. Their relative value is not worth debating, given that a single flexible formation rooted in principle is best.

In training officers, it is important to intermittently change who your students are teamed up with. Shuffle up the groups. By doing this you avoid students becoming familiar with each other's tendencies, which can create bad habits and cause them to stray from their principles. By regrouping your teams, you *force a dependence on the system* and its operating principles. This not only reinforces those principles but prepares students for the field, when they will be working with different people, maybe even people they don't know. This is a huge advantage of using consistent training practices, and recombining your teams will reinforce the behaviour you want them to internalize.

Residential Searches

The figures and examples we've discussed thus far are a little sterile but typical of what you might encounter moving through a commercial property or school. They are excellent training environments to begin learning this new concept of a flexible formation, but its true value is yet to come. Let's move into some different environments and observe how the students respond.

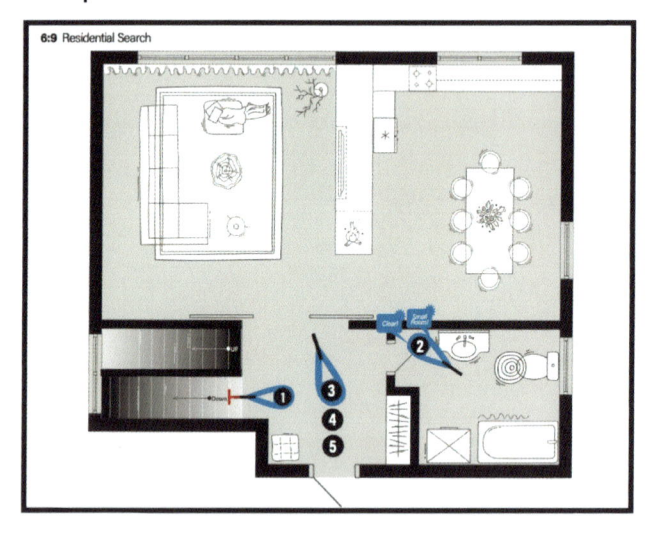

6:9 Residential Search

Once again, an instructional discussion should begin the process. Excluding topics like containment, breaching, and external team movement, the instructor touches on the basic principles of Tactical Thinking, the Thought Process, reading-off team members, squeezing up, and verbally stating intentions. Remember that these discussions are the key to involving students in training. They instil a level of understanding that cannot be achieved by giving students the answers.

This level of understanding is crucial, as students take on unknown challenges in the field and you cannot be there to provide them with answers. The key to these instructional discussions is to recognize when they are counterproductive. That is, once the students understand what they are supposed to do, let them start drilling. There comes a time when their eyes glaze over and the information stops reaching its intended target. A teacher needs to identify that moment and start drilling the repetitions.

In **Figure 6.9**, we see the officers at the point of entry. Again, begin with an instructional discussion to ensure each team member is making the appropriate decisions, and most importantly, for the right reasons. Note that the first officer through the door has appropriately decided to post on the basement stairwell. The officer reading off her movement has recognized that posting is a one-person job and becomes the lead officer, moving into the residence. The second officer may opt to proceed directly into the residence, depending on the information he has. Quite often, searches are intelligence driven, and what is on the main floor may represent a higher priority than the rest of the residence.

Residential searches present some unique challenges. Spaces are usually confined and there are adjoining rooms. Sometimes officers may just stay in their PRD while other officers move through that room into the next, if there are no blatant uncleared problem areas they need to pass. Another challenge is that if an officer has contact with a person to be detained, she may just prone that person out and let other officers pass through, depending on the compliance of the suspect, for a more efficient search. These challenges are more pertinent in a more dynamic style of entry, such as that of a tactical unit where preventing the destruction of

6:10 Residential Search

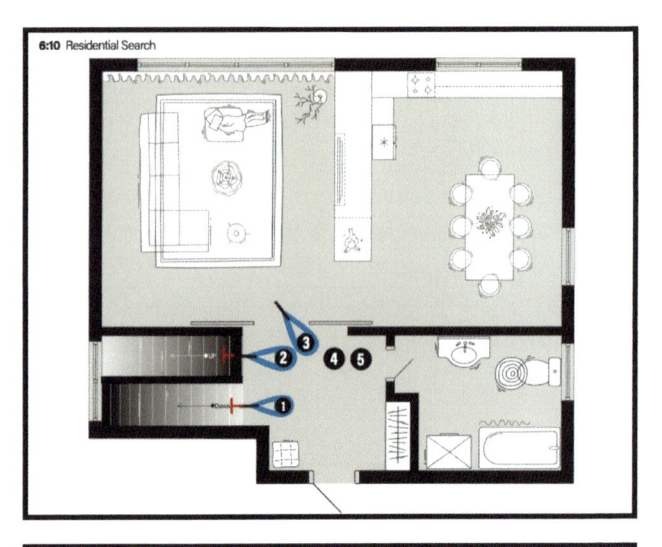

6:11 Residential Search

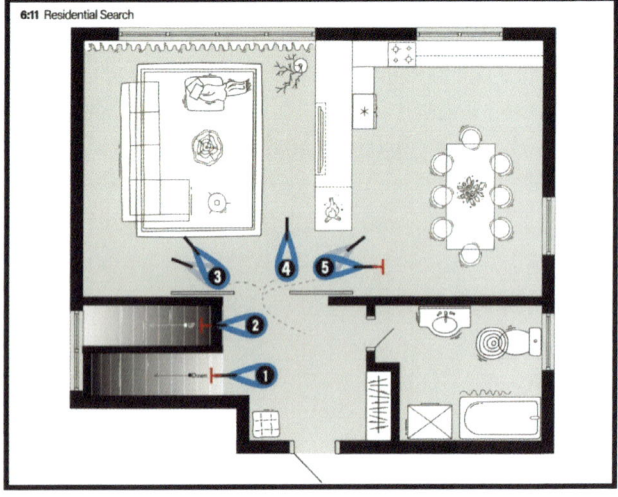

evidence or controlling suspects before they arm themselves are priorities. As the officers move through the residence, they come to the stairs leading to the upper level (**Figure 6.10**). In most residences, upstairs is where the bedrooms are. The second officer has appropriately chosen to post on those stairs, but it could just as easily be any member of the team. Two members clear the main floor living room and as you can see, all team members are now occupied, with the last available member posting on the kitchen area (**Figure 6.11**). Once the main floor is completed, the members will stack up on one of their posts and clear the remaining areas. Which one they decide to do first is intelligence driven.

This entry could be done in a completely different way and still be based on sound principles. If the intelligence was that the known target was downstairs or if people were in danger downstairs, the officers' movements would look quite different. For instance, they may have all proceeded downstairs while one officer remained posted on the rest of the residence, as in **Figure 6.12**. As you can see from the peripheral field graphic and scanning icon, one officer can quite capably be responsible for a large area.

6:12 Residential Search

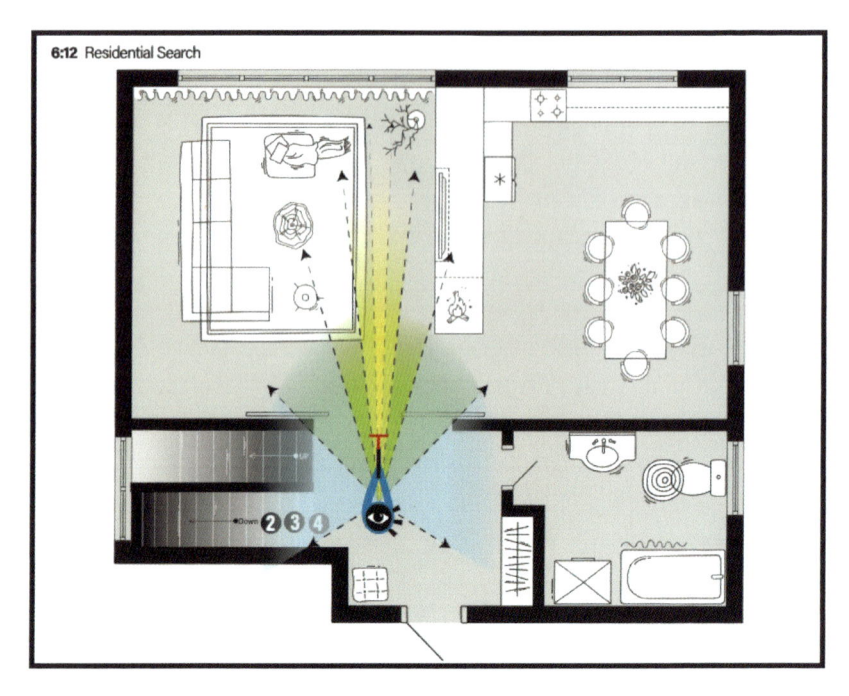

This is how you train the flexible formation—by relieving team members of rigidity and empowering them with sound principles, knowledge, and objectives. There is no end to the different configurations of structures police officers have to search, which is why this approach to training is focused on internalizing key principles. This investment will yield huge returns when your students approach unknowns in the field, because you will have given them a toolbox, an answer key to solving those problems themselves.

But the greatest benefit to the flexible formation has yet to be seen, when it is used to respond to the most stressful of all events, the active killing in progress.

7

Active Killing

*We do not rise to the level of
our expectations,
we fall to the level of our
training.*

Archilochus

My greatest motivation for sharing this single formation theory is the law enforcement community's flawed solution to the recent epidemic of mass murder events such as school shootings.

From a tactical perspective, the reaction from North American police organizations to the increase of mass murders has been to develop formations specifically designed to respond to these killings in progress and end them. These formations are not used otherwise. Different formations have been developed, and attractive and expensive training programs have been marketed for law enforcement services to adopt. If the goal is to reduce the potential liability of police services, this has been a successful strategy. If police services are ever criticized for their response when such horrible events occur in their jurisdiction, they can answer that they have the most modern and effective system available, and that they acted in accordance with that training. The problem is that these systems are *not* effective. Although they look great on paper, they have very little chance of success in the field, for several reasons.

As a trainer, I have seen the deterioration of inadequately trained skill sets under stress, and there is no more stressful event than responding to a mass murder. In times of stress, we need to fall back on the skills we have internalized and already know inside and out, not hope to miraculously access skills that are markedly different from everything else in our training curriculum in language and principle; skills that we've only trained for eight hours in recruit class and inadequately, if at all, since then.

Instead, more effort needs to be devoted to realistic training. "Realistic" refers not only to the practical limitations of training officers discussed in chapter 1, but more importantly, officers need to be trained and prepared for the situations they are *actually* going to be responding to. Are we training officers for what is going on in the real world? Let's look at the question another way.

Where Is the Evidence That What We Are Training Is Working?

To answer this critical question, I draw upon the incredible life work of the most dedicated researcher in this field. Ron Borsch is the founder and manager of the PACT Consultant Group. He served 30 years in the Bedford (Ohio) Police Department, and for 17 years was manager and trainer at the SEALE Regional Police Training Academy, attended by officers from 10 states. His research into rapid mass murders is exceptional and his willingness to share what he calls "life-saving information" is commendable. Borsch's basic definition of a **rapid mass murder** is four or more murders or attempted murders in a public place within 20 minutes. I've had the pleasure of communicating directly with Mr. Borsch, and his research should have police organizations everywhere questioning their approach to dealing with active killings. I assume you would like your training to reflect reality, so absorb this.

Borsch has supplied research from approximately 270 known active killings between 1975 and late 2018. Borsch's research is primarily in the United States, and he has coined the term "stopwatch of death." This stopwatch begins when the killing in a mass murder starts and ends when the killing stops. You may be shocked to hear that for events where this time is known, the average stopwatch of death lasts less than six minutes. This average can be a little misleading, as a good deal of these killings are over in two minutes or less—*that* is what we need to prepare for.

These are disturbing statistics, considering that the most widely accepted active killing intervention programs are built on the hope that a group of officers will respond in time to end the killing. This is a faint hope at best. The likelihood of an off-site group response to an active killing as an intervention strategy is almost impossible.

In fact, out of the 270 mass murders that Borsch has analyzed to date, there is only one example he is aware of that was successfully stopped by a team of four or more officers. In this incident, university police responded with two 4-person teams. This is very rare and they were probably within close proximity when the killing began. A formation response to an active killing is an anomaly, not a norm, a 1:270 ratio to be exact. That's 0.37%. We are investing our money, effort, training time, hopes, and dreams in the 0.37% chance that we will have a team of four or more officers to enter a rapid mass murder in progress.

The most effective police intervention strategy has been and continues to be that of a solo officer arriving on scene and going after the active killer by himself, as opposed to waiting to round up a posse. "Tactical loitering," as it were, has almost always failed to stop the murdering. If the murdering is still going on when the first officer arrives on scene, he will be far more successful at stopping the murdering if he acts aggressively, immediately, and alone. The masses of responding officers coming to the scene will assist, but it is the action or distraction by the first officer who initiates the contact that stops the killing.

The reality is that half of these 270 rapid mass murders studied by Borsch weren't stopped at all; these murders were self-aborted by departure, surrender, or suicide of the murderer. Out of the 135 mass murders that were stopped by intervention, approximately 70% of these were ended by on-site, mostly unarmed citizens, and 30% were ended by police intervention.

This means that out of 270 events, only 42 (approximately 15% overall) were ended by police. Out of these 42 events ended by police, 70% were terminated due to the valiant efforts of a solo officer acting aggressively, followed by 12 times (approximately 4.5% overall) where two or three officers ended the threat, and finally the unbelievable 1 instance out of 270 case studies where four officers or more were rounded up to end the event.

What Are We Training Our People For?

If officers are trained to respond to an active killing with a formation of four or five members, they're not being trained for reality. They are being trained for the red sliver represented at the top of the following pie graph.

These numbers are the reality. We should be training officers to enter aggressively and begin hunting for the killer, alone if necessary. We should train officers how to locate the killer by identifying what Borsch calls contact clues: sights, sounds, and smells such as cordite, blood, bullet cases, or fecal matter.

Cause of Active Killing Terminations (270 Case Studies)

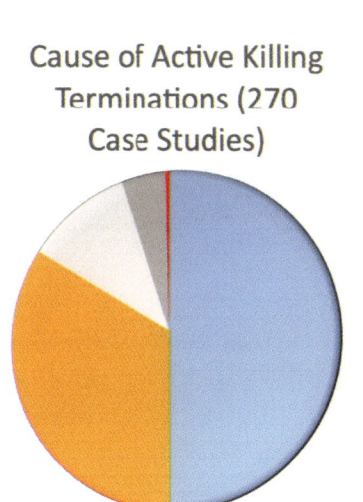

- Self Aborted
- Police Initiated-Solo Officer
- Police Initiated-4plus
- On Scene Civilian
- Police Initiated-2 or 3 Officers

We should be teaching officers how to competently operate in a tactically sound manner, both on their own and in small groups of two or three, because that is how they *will* be operating. There needs to be a strong focus on linking up with other officers who will be entering the murder scene from alternate points of entry and using a simple and flexible formation structure that will allow for this.

When I talk about reality-based or more realistic training, this is what I am referring to. The reality is that we need to be training our officers for the highest-probability situations. We need to spend 99% of our training time for 99% of reality, not 99% of our training time preparing for the 0.37% reality. *This is the active killer fallacy*. Yet the majority of expensive training programs on the market spend most of their training time focused on group formation responses, which has stopped the murdering only 1 time in 270 instances since 1975.

The focus of our training needs to be on empowering individual officers with an intrinsic understanding of the tactical principles and thinking models presented in this primer, so they are prepared to make good decisions while acting alone or in a very small group.

Active killings are a phenomenon with no easy solutions, but we can all agree that a police response will not solve the bigger issue. By the time someone has begun actively killing people, the situation has spiralled out of control. Expecting police to solve active killings or mass murder is like putting a band-aid on a compound fracture. Mass murders are a complex societal problem and require a societal response.

If organizations want to be prepared for a mass murder in their home town, they do not need to spend more time and money sending their members out of town for slick training programs that will rarely, if ever, be used. Although I am not a subject matter expert in rapid mass murders, I have observed promising initiatives and concerning shortcomings that are worth considering:

- Police organizations, hospitals, and emergency medical services need to be prepared for a massive medical response to deal with the overwhelming casualties that occur in incidents such as mass murders, and have a coordinated strategy so that

area hospitals are aware of the impending influx of wounded and have an emergency plan in place.
- Police organizations need more people like Sergeant Shane Cooke of the Winnipeg Police Service's Tactical Support Team (Canada), who created a Tactical Emergency Medical Support Team (TEMS) consisting of hand-selected paramedics who train regularly with that service's tactical unit to operate seamlessly and interdepartmentally at high-risk events. This team is trained to act in concert with tactical teams and provide emergency field trauma casualty care and triage to the wounded.
- Law enforcement organizations, school administrators, prominent business moguls, and employers need to meet and identify red flag behaviour in individuals so that when it is identified and quantified, it can be acted upon and hopefully prevent some of these tragedies. Prevention is the key.
- Schools need to hold more lock-down drills.
- Society in general needs to be more tuned in to what is going on. Denial is the killer. Threat cues need to be measured, labeled, and taken seriously.
- Police organizations need to have more table-top exercises so that they can effectively manage the chaotic scene in the aftermath of a mass murder. Do we have an effective emergency scene management plan that enables us to expeditiously triage, prioritize, and evacuate the wounded? Do we have a plan to secure the scene from the throngs of irate or terrified family members arriving on scene? Do we have a plan in place to screen the survivors running out of a

scene, in order to prevent possible suspects from masquerading among them?

What Needs to Change

These and other interventions are the subject of much debate, but whatever we decide, our solutions and strategies need to be based in evidence, not guesswork and speculation.

One thing is certain from a police response option: if we are focusing most of our training time employing a tactical formation as an intervention strategy for the 1 in 270 chance and counting that we'll use it in the field, we're failing epically. We need to use the precious training time we're afforded to build on what we already know and enhance it to manage the challenges that are unique to each emergency. We cannot throw everything we have trained so hard to build out the window because some uninformed individuals think that responding to an active killer is a whole different animal and we need a completely different approach. These are the times that we need to fall back on what we are already well-versed in and make the minor adjustments to address the new challenges.

In using a flexible formation, we have already seen the advantages of maintaining the integrity of the formation by instilling team members with the principles to adapt to a changing environment. Adapting the formation in response to a homicide in progress is no different.

A fact that is sometimes overlooked is that the slow and methodical search can change into an imminent threat to life or homicide in progress in a heartbeat—and then back again. For example, if our team is clearing a place where nobody is actively being killed, that is, the threat is not imminent, then we are conducting a slow and methodical search. If suddenly the situation changes, such as gun shots sounding or other indications somebody is being killed, we proceed directly to the threat. In an active killing situation, the possibility of switching from one mode to the next in a single event is much more likely than the dynamics not changing. And given that, the idea of changing our formation from one type, such as a column formation, back to a five-person tethered formation and back to a file formation is simply preposterous. Instead, we need to adopt a single formation, a team of tactically sound and principle-based members capable of adapting to the changes in mission and environment.

How We Need to Train

Formation training should begin with a single officer response, not a group response, since the reality is that this is the most likely option and has had the most success of all police-initiated mass murder terminations. As trainers, we need to show what a solo officer needs to do differently to apply the principles we've talked about thus far. The next step is to begin adding officers to the formation and demonstrating the construction of the flexible amoeba formation, and finally, various linkup strategies. Given the low probability of a team response to an active killing, adapting our formation to the changes in stimulus needs to be the focus of training, as opposed to assuming new formations.

The outline in **Figure 7.1** is typical of a school structure and shows an officer arriving on scene. His priority should be to *stop, look, listen and smell* for the contact clues mentioned earlier and begin moving toward the threat. The officer is alone now, so if there is no imminent threat to life or people actively being murdered, he should wait for additional resources and proceed in a building search fashion and start addressing the medical concerns of the wounded. The killer may have taken his own life, or the situation may have changed to a hostage taking. But if there is active killing, the officer needs to get to that threat and eliminate it as quickly as possible and by himself.

During training, this is an excellent time for another instructional discussion in which you can ask the students questions to ensure they understand the urgency as well as to ensure they are embracing and adapting what they have learned thus far to this new situation.

Instructor: What is your objective?

Student: To eliminate the threat.

Instructor: Should you clear rooms as you go to the threat?

Student: No. People are being killed. I need to get there.

Instructor: What are your areas of responsibility?

Student: Everything.

Instructor: What contact clues have you found?

Student: I hear gunfire and see bullet casings and blood leading down to the room at the end of the hall, and I can hear people screaming down there.

Instructor: If there is no imminent threat to life, what do you do?

Student: Wait for backup.

Instructor: Do you cut the pie slowly and methodically on that doorway?

Student: I'll cut the pie on the doorway, just dynamically.

Instructor: Why?

Student: Because the second or two it takes to cut the pie statically could mean another person killed.

Instructor: Isn't there more personal risk to cutting to pie more dynamically?

Student: Possibly. But that's a risk I'll have to take because people are being killed.

7:1 School—One Officer with Imminent Threat to Life

Instructor: What is your objective?
Student: To eliminate the threat.

Instructor: Do you want to clear rooms as you go to the threat?
Student: No. People are being killed. I need to get there.

Instructor: What are your areas of responsibility?
Student: Everything

Instructor: What contact clues have you found?
Student: I hear gunfire and see bullet casings and blood leading dow to the room at the end of the hall and I can hear people screaming down there.

Instructor: If there is no imminent threat to life, what do you do?
Student: Wait for back up.

Instructor: Will you cut the pie slowly and methodically on that doorway?
Student: I'll still cut the pie on the doorway, just dynamically.

Instructor: Why?
Student: Because the second or two it takes to cut the pie slowly could be another person killed.

Instructor: Isn't that dangerous?
Student: Yes. But there's an imminent threat to life so we need to.

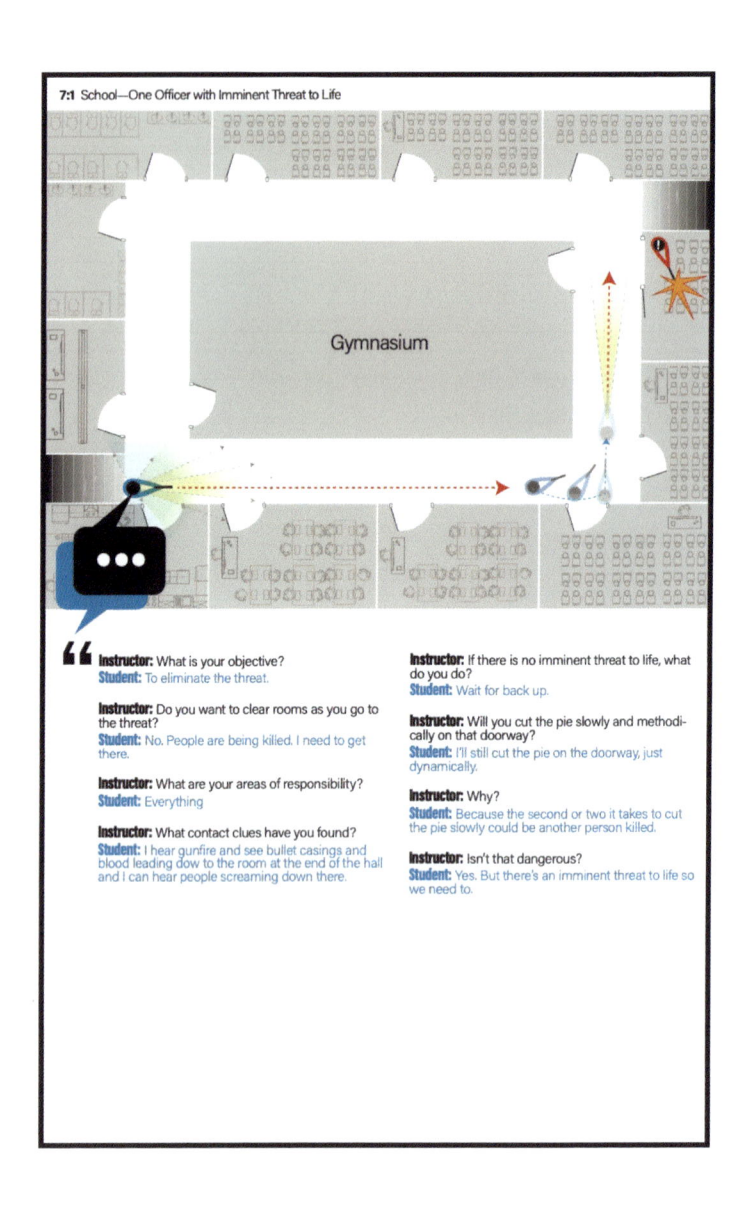

The benefit of rote repetitions and instilling principles will now pay off as you see students applying them. Once the Thought Process has been verified through instructional discussion, allow the student to proceed.

The tactical thinking models we've discussed in earlier chapters do not change. The only thing that changes is that the officer is solely responsible for all AORs, so he may choose to scan rooms as he passes and over his shoulder to address rear security. But remember, if this officer is aware of where the threat is, alternate AORS, such as rear security, are just a precaution and should not deter him from his primary objective. Scanning is essential because of the effects of high stress on the peripheral field. The officer may choose to employ some of the strategies described in chapter 4 to manage the effects of the stress, such as tactical breathing to lower the heart rate.

Quite often students will be hesitant to run into battle and eliminate the threat. They will cite various reasons, but the real reason is because they are scared. It's a reasonable emotion under the circumstances. My training intervention for this hesitancy is to ask them a simple question: What if it was your child in that classroom and she was the next to be executed? Or your mother in her workplace? That usually puts things in perspective for most students.

Once the officer eliminates the threat, which for the purposes of this training primer is elementary at this point, the drill should be repeated as many times as possible. Observational learning, minimal discussion, and many repetitions are the objective. Add an officer with each evolution of the training exercise to make two and three-person formations, and occasionally add one from an alternate point of entry to practice linking up with others.

Employ instructional discussion to ensure each officer is thinking with a principle-based and tactically sound mind-set.

Ultimately, a larger formation should be trained and integrated, even though the likelihood of using that to end a threat is minimal. The primary reason we want to continue to train in groups of five or more is because the probability of having to transform from a slow and methodical building search to responding to a homicide in progress, and back again, is very likely. For example, if the threat has been eliminated and now officers need to clear the rest of the area, or if there is no active killing but the location of the threat is not known, a slow, methodical search will ensue.

However, when we begin training a single officer response and gradually increase the numbers, as we have done thus far, our training is more congruent with what occurs in the field. The most successful police intervention is a solo officer response, so our training time should be delegated to reflect that.

A sample training outline would look something like the one on the following page:

Drill	Technique	Time
1	- solo officer - instructional discussion - AORs, direct to threat, dynamic cutting the pie	2 hours
2	- 2 officers, same as above - adjust AORs (rear security)	2 hours
3	- 3 officers, same as drills 1 and 2 - adjust AORs	2 hours
4	- 4 officers, same as above - adjust AORs	1 hour
5	- 5+ officers (all the above) - link-ups with officers from other points of entry - adapt formation from direct to threat to slow building search (once threat is eliminated)	1 hour

Notice that in this outline, the time allotted to complete each training evolution is reversed from the training outline for building search training (chapter 6). In the case of training for an active killer event, the drills begin with, and more time is allotted for, the single officer to make the adjustment and adapt the principles learned while acting alone. At the risk of overstating it, this is by design, to reflect the statistical likelihood of use in the field. This is how we design our training to mirror reality.

Furthermore, with a restricted time frame to train the larger formations comes a reliance on the basics we have already ingrained in our students. This forces them to fall back on their existing training and adapt it to the new challenges, enhancing the overall efficacy of our training and practice through consistency.

Known Threat versus Unknown Threat

In addition to our training reflecting reality, when we are training in formation, we should train both for when the threat is known and officers are proceeding directly to that threat, in the unlikely event that occurs, and for the likelier event that a group of officers are conducting a slow methodical building search when the mission changes and an imminent threat to life occurs.

Let's touch on both.

When a threat to life arises but the location of the threat is unknown, officers do not need to transform into a new formation, such as a five-person tethered formation or a Tee, Vee, or diamond formation (revisit **Figure 6.8**), they just need to use the tactical thinking that they've already been taught and critically self-assess their tactics. Are they employing tactics that will shorten their tactical thought process and lengthen the suspect's thought process accordingly? And since team members are now passing uncleared problem areas, AORs need to be adjusted.

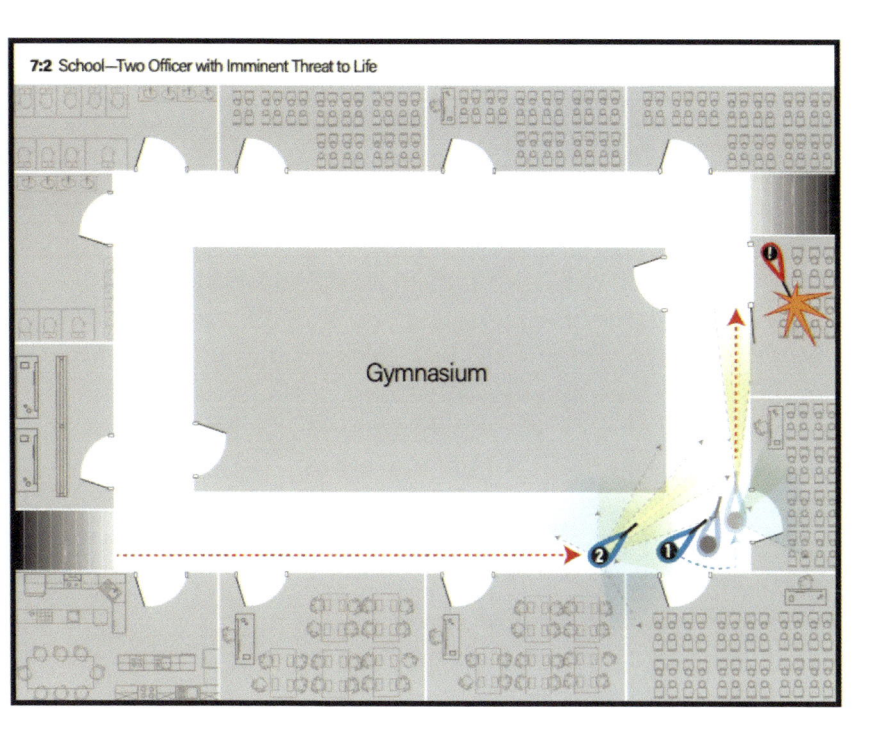

7:2 School—Two Officer with Imminent Threat to Life

If you are training your members to do this, begin with an instructional discussion with each of them to ensure that they are acting in accordance with the principles taught and are making tactically sound decisions. If team members are moving in cohesion and using constant verbal and non-verbal communication with each other, covering of all their AORs while moving directly to eliminate the threat, they deserve praise and reward for doing well, given their varying aptitudes and the limited training time that they've had.

As **Figure 7.2** illustrates, the first team member has recognized an imminent threat to life and begins moving to the threat. Note that the beams that reflect the field of vision have been slightly reduced. A narrowed visual field and loss of peripheral vision are common in times of high stress, as we've discussed, and this must be compensated for by constantly scanning.

In **Figure 7.3**, the second member of the team has realized that two guns down range are better than one, so to enhance her ability to react, she positions herself just off the lead officer's flank. This enables her to a gain a better vantage on her AORs. The third officer joining will recognize that they are now passing uncleared areas, so he employs scanning and adjusts his AORs accordingly. Remember that in a slow and methodical building search, team members clear everything as they pass it, the exception being what they've posted on. Now the officers are moving directly to the threat, so every member of the team needs to be aware of this and make adjustments.

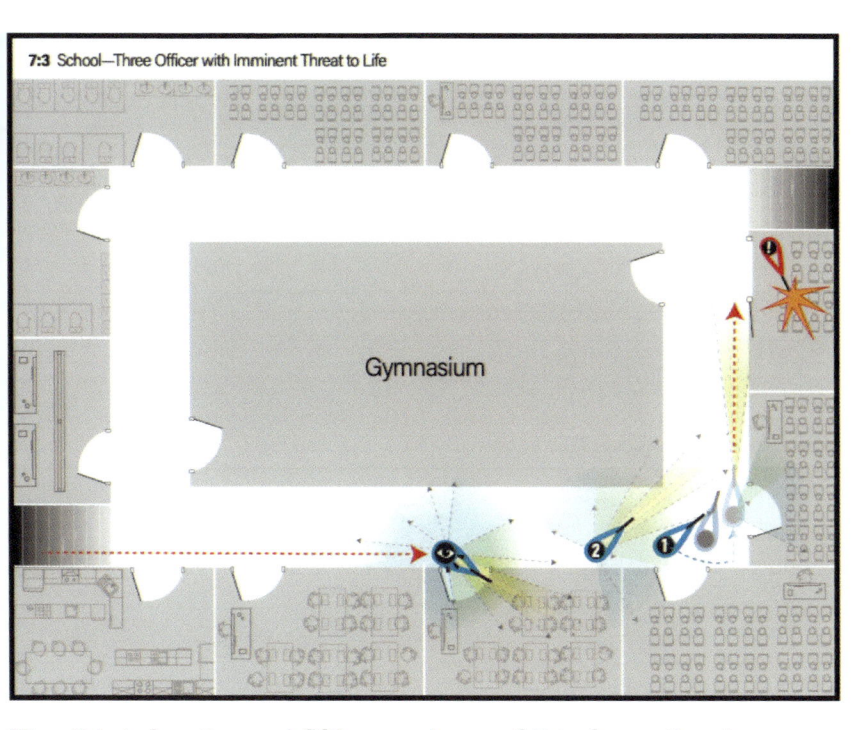

7:3 School—Three Officer with Imminent Threat to Life

The third, fourth, and fifth members of this formation have made the same adjustments as the second member (**Figure 7.4**), but the last officer of the formation has an AOR unlike his teammates: rear security. Rear security is an important AOR, especially since the team is not clearing as it goes, however, it should be handled relative to other priorities. I have seen some tactical formations in which one or more members at the rear of the formation are encouraged to walk or run backward to enhance the coverage on the rear AOR. However, I've never seen anyone running backward to the sound of gunfire in all my years of tactical training and research. I refuse to train it.

Of course, rear security is a high priority, but realistically, if team members are moving in this fashion to begin with it means that there is imminent threat to life. But again, if we know there is an imminent threat to life, if we have identified the location of that threat and are moving toward it, rear security is more of a precaution in the less likely event of a second threat. Rear security needs to be addressed, but with proper perspective. Team members can pay attention to the perceived threat behind them but much more so, **give priority to the real threat** ahead. The one thing officers should *not* do is take themselves out of the fight by walking or running backward, as some training programs teach.

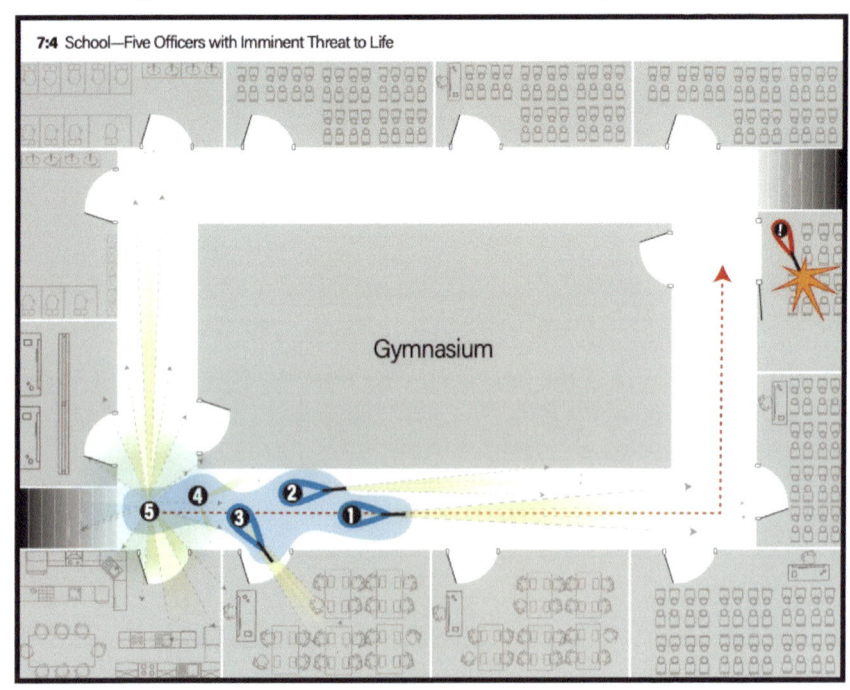

7:4 School—Five Officers with Imminent Threat to Life

This is the reason to train the last member of the formation, while responding to an imminent threat, to move forward in a natural manner while checking over his shoulders constantly, as opposed to running backward or some nonsense. This

148

way he is not going to stumble over team members, possibly fall, and take himself out of the fight. At a point when the team needs to stop to reassess its movement is the most appropriate time for the rear security member to take a committed view of his AOR.

In **Figure 7.4**, when the formation begins to move and change shape, it looks like an amoeba, doesn't it?

A beautiful aspect of a simple and flexible formation such as this, and likewise with the slow building search, is its ability to move in any direction. The built-in correctors and adjusters such as the read off allow this to happen. For example, in **Figure 7.5**, if the last member of the formation encounters a threat in his AOR, he will announce he has contact or begin issuing verbal commands to the suspect, and the other members of the formation will react accordingly. The rear officer has now become the lead officer. The second officer will now read-off his movements, the third and fourth officers will adjust accordingly, and the former lead officer is now the last member of the formation and responsible for rear security.

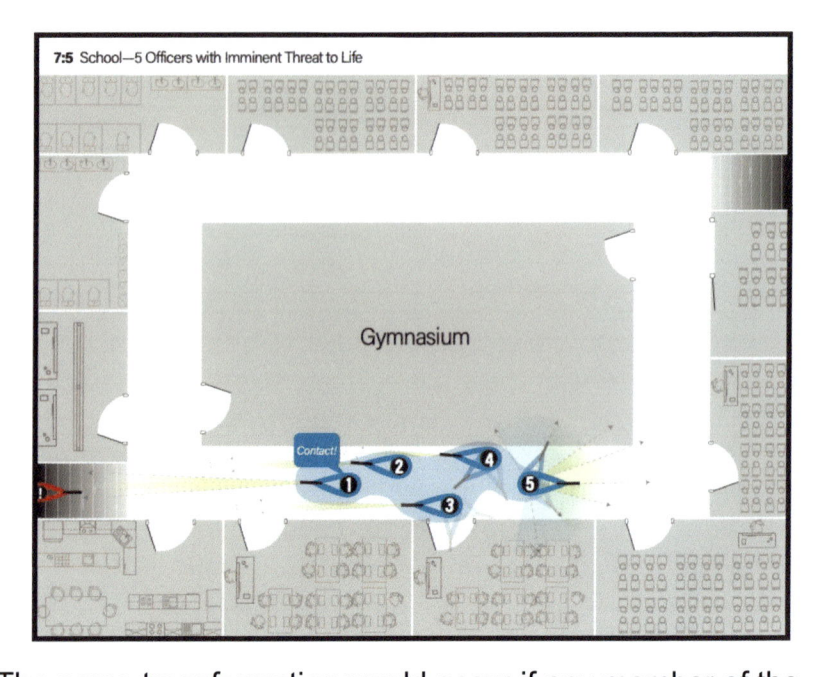

7:5 School—5 Officers with Imminent Threat to Life

Gymnasium

The same transformation would occur if any member of the formation picks up on a threat before the others do. In **Figure 7.6**, the second officer has picked up on the threat and has contact with the suspect. She begins issuing verbal commands and the rest of the team adjusts optimally and accordingly. This would not be as simple as if she were the lead or rear member of the formation, as it is not always predetermined who will read off the contact officer's movement. But just like calling for a fly ball, the communication and dedicated actions of one member will enhance the adjustment of the rest. In this figure, the team adheres to its' principles and makes the appropriate adjustments. In **Figure 7.7**, the fifth officer has picked up the threat, so obviously he would address it. Then the other team members would adhere to their principles and adjust accordingly.

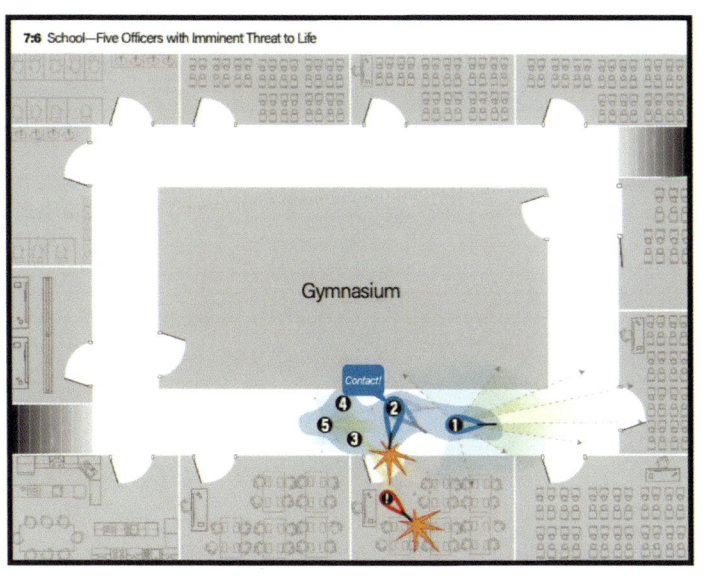

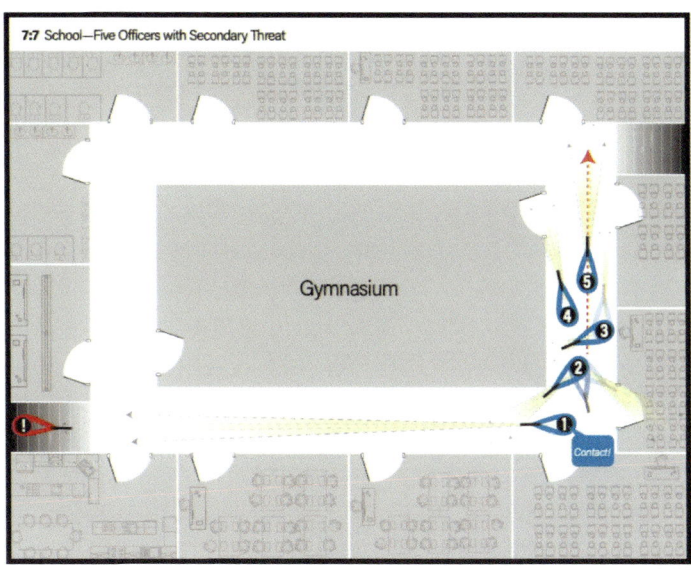

7:6 School—Five Officers with Imminent Threat to Life

7:7 School—Five Officers with Secondary Threat

I would conduct additional drills in the identical manner, except with the change in stimulus that we are now conducting a search in which the threat has not been located and is not imminent. Again, the starting point should be an instructional discussion, but ultimately it would be treated like a slow and methodical building search.

Situations can change in a heartbeat. Rather than adopting a new formation, set of commands, and principles, we can be comforted in knowing that we only need to adapt what we already know and know well. We need to be as consistent as possible.

With the training your students have received up until this phase—the instructional discussions, heavy emphasis on principle-based decision-making, tactical thinking, and repetitive training—the *gaps*, or AORs that need to be covered off will begin to jump out at your officers in an obvious way. When this has begun to happen, your students are mastering what you need them to: the essence of tactical thinking and competence.

Another advantage to keeping our formation simple and consistent is that it always becomes our reset when the situation gets a little crazy. In a mass murder or critical incident where there are masses of innocent people trying to flee the building, literally running for their lives, or even if the threat has been eliminated and officers are searching while survivors are evacuating (**Figure 7.8**), *the amoebic-like* flexible formation can quickly contract into its *column-like* starting point to avoid being broken up as can happen with some other formations (**Figure 7.9**), and then expand again once the masses pass.

7:8 Maintaining Formation in a Flee Situation

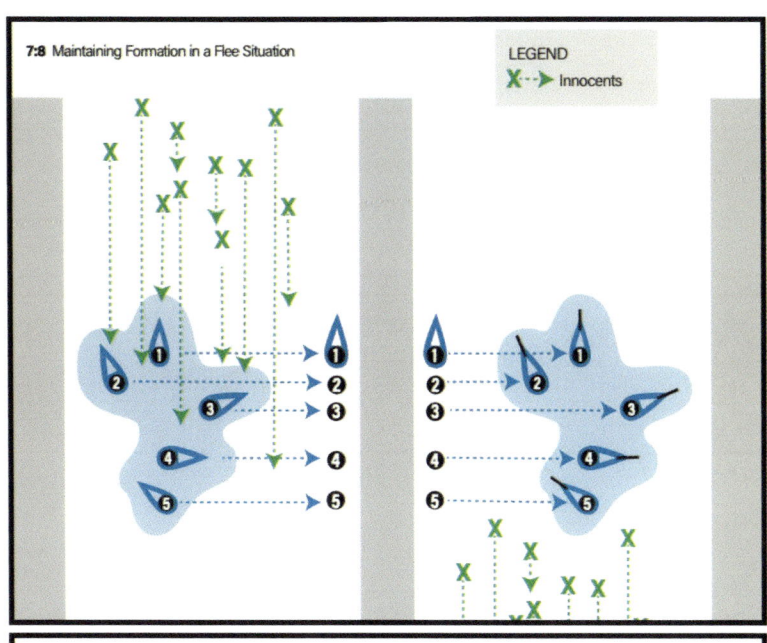

LEGEND
X --▶ Innocents

7:9 Unsuitable Formations in a Flee Situation

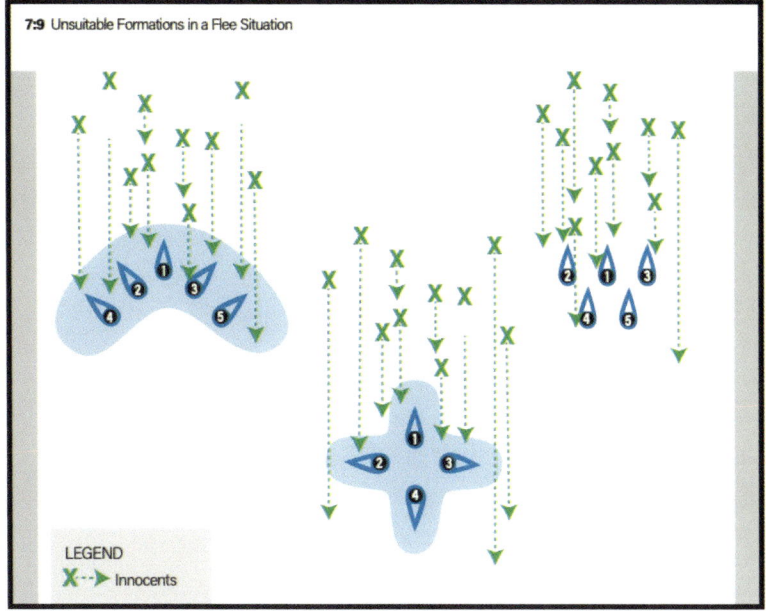

LEGEND
X --▶ Innocents

153

7-10 Scanning & breathing

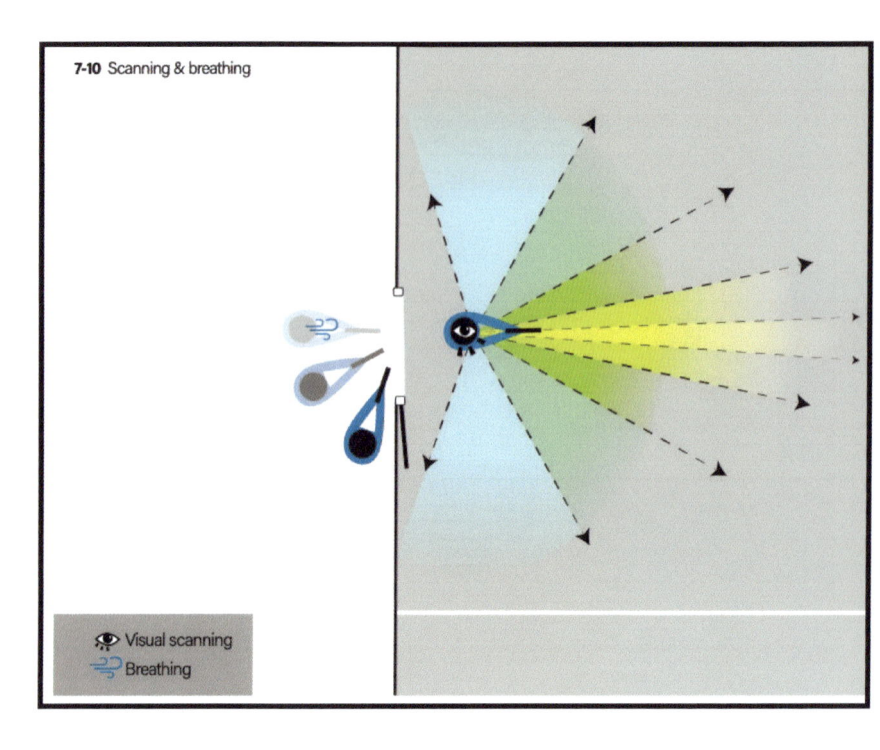

👁 Visual scanning
💨 Breathing

Single Officer Room Entry

An officer entering a room by himself is unfavourable but may be necessary, such as in a response to a homicide in progress. If a solo-officer room entry is to be conducted and the threat is not immediately evident, then the officer must rely heavily on his peripheral vision at the point of entry to alert him of any potential threats, especially if the room has a center-feeding doorway, as is the case in **Figure 7.10**. As we learned in chapter 4, this is an issue because of the physiological effects of stress and the loss of peripheral vision. (Note the loss of peripheral vision represented in the diagrams earlier in this chapter).

Circumstances such as these are when stress management tools become an asset. When approaching the doorway or entering the room would be an excellent time to employ some tactical breathing and scanning to restore the peripheral vision and mitigate tunnel vision (**Figure 7.10**). And remember that cutting the pie (dynamically) and observing inside the room begins before arriving at the point of entry. The more information we have about what awaits us the better, and every sight, sound, and smell will provide valuable information.

The best case scenario is when an officer approaches a corner-feeding doorway, either by herself or as the lead officer, as shown in **Figure 7.11**. With this configuration, the officer can observe a good portion of the area she is entering prior to penetrating the room. The worst-case scenario is the reverse room configuration, as shown in **Figure 7.12**. Remember that cutting the pie on these points of entry can be done very quickly when required. It's not necessary to throw these techniques out the window in times of urgency, just hit the fast-forward button.

7-11 Corner Doorway—Best Scenario

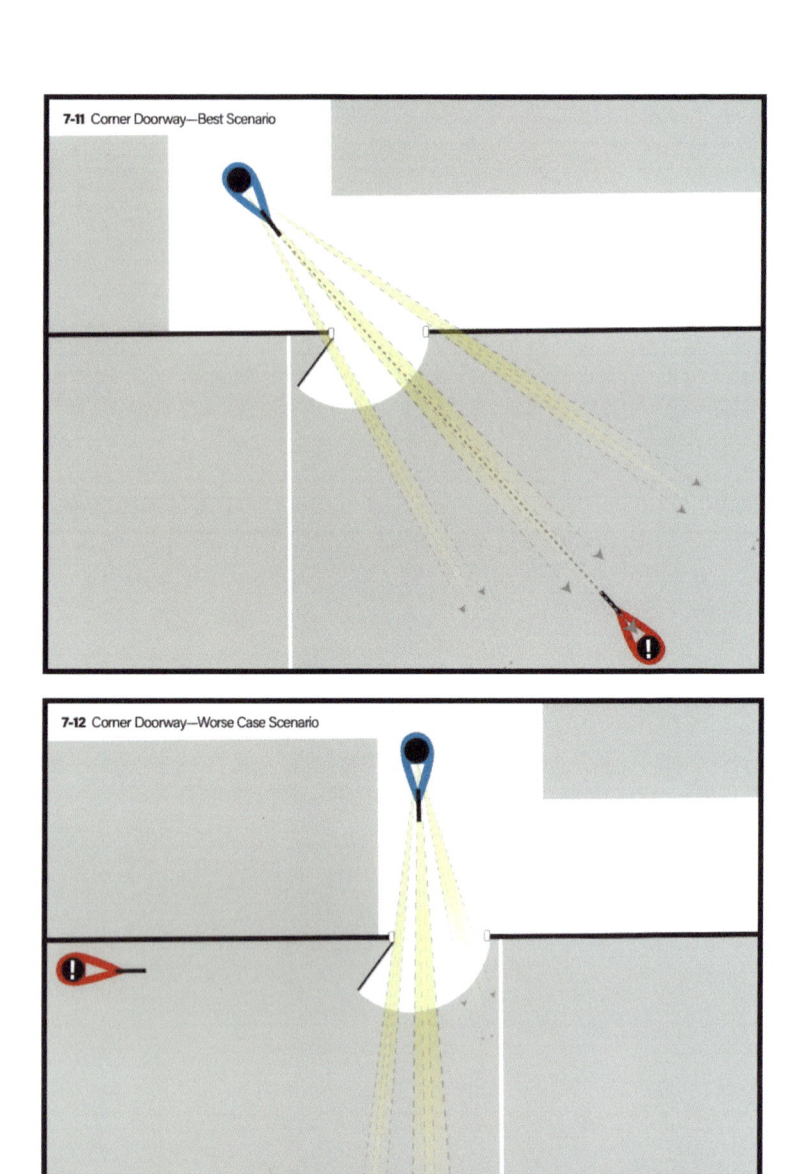

7-12 Corner Doorway—Worse Case Scenario

156

In conclusion, in order for officers to deal with these kinds of chaotic situations, we need to provide them with a simple set of skills that they can fall back on with little conscious thought. To expect officers to adapt to a different formation amid a life-and-death encounter, with the minimal training time they are allotted, would be an irresponsible and epic failing in our curriculum.

Furthermore, by eliminating different formations that are poorly designed for the realities faced by officers in training and in the field, we gain valuable time to reinforce the basics.

This is the mission of this entire training primer: implementing an exhaustive repetition of simple, principle-based techniques and tactical thought processes to create a system that will be accessible, adaptable, and effective in the highest-probability encounters, as opposed to creating complex tactics that will confuse students, be inaccessible to officers due to training constraints, and are designed for unlikely possibilities.

8

Pushing Forward

Never interrupt your enemy when he is making a mistake.
Napoleon Bonaparte

The concept of a single flexible formation to respond to a variety of different situations is a relatively simple, seemingly obvious notion, but for some reason the simplicity continues to elude us. Quite frankly, there is far too much pontification with a marker and a grease board, drawing Xs and Os and constructing intricate tactical solutions to an infinite number of possibilities, and not enough time spent on *repping the basics.*

Perfect solutions masterfully handcrafted in a static environment don't always look as cool in an actual fight as they do on the chalkboard. As Mike Tyson said, *"Everyone has a plan until they get hit."* You need one or two devastating punches in your arsenal, and you can't mind getting punched in the face to optimize your chances in a street fight. Good tactics are like this. They should be designed for the ugly fights, not for their aesthetic appeal.

You don't perfect the jump shot from drawing theory on a grease board. You perfect the jump shot by throwing the ball on a court, at a net, thousands of times. Once every couple of hundred repetitions, a coach will come along and give you a pointer, and then you throw the ball a few hundred more times. Repetition–tweak–repetition–tweak. It develops over time. The only problem is it's extremely boring and the lesson plan does not look very impressive. But it works.

A friend of mine from the military special forces community and I were discussing the importance of simplicity in tactics when he put it quite aptly: *"You don't see guys in round five of an Ultimate Fighting Championship fight executing a flying double reverse roundhouse kick."* That says it all. You don't see fancy techniques, because they do not hold up under periods of exhaustion or high stress. You see two exhausted and battered warriors using gross motor skill techniques and punching and kicking the living crap out of each other. I've been involved in martial arts my entire life and I've picked up some nifty techniques over the years, but whenever I've got into a fight on the street, I go back to the same three or four techniques that I know are going to give me the best chance to win. These are techniques that suit me personally, and ones I've rehearsed thousands of times.

Why? Because simplicity works.

But we police officers and police trainers are an interesting breed, and we just can't seem to quit messing with things. Methinks ego is sometimes the culprit. Striving for improvement and progress is essential, but equally important to remember is that *if it's not broke, don't fix it.*

A single flexible formation, if trained properly, will give officers a simple and effective skill set that they will be able to access under stress and that will give them the best chance for success. If we ingrain in them the operating principles that I've discussed in this primer, our officers will be empowered to solve problems in a tactically sound matter when those unforeseen challenges emerge.

Adopting Consistency

Aside from taking a principle-based approach to tactical formation training, trainers can and *should* employ those same principles in every aspect of their curriculum—handcuffing, subject control, firearms training, etc.—for faster learning and better retention of all the programs by way of consistency.

It is not only important that we use consistent principles and language within our own areas of responsibilities—such as defensive tactics, firearms, police vehicle operations, or the tactical unit—but crucial that these units' training programs are consistent with each other. There is no reason the tactical unit needs to operate any differently than the frontline officers of an organization, or any specialty unit for that matter. The easiest way to confuse people is to change their language.

There will be different adaptations and different levels of skill competency between tactical and uniformed operations that come with use or disuse, function or training, but on the level of basic principles, we should all have the same starting point. There should be no difference. When you strive for this consistency within your organization, you have the ability to integrate your resources. Some situations are going to be dealt with solely by a tactical unit and others, solely by uniformed operations. Many situations will be dealt with by both, so that cohesion should be as seamless as possible. At times there may only be two tactical officers available on the street, so rather than waiting around for the rest of the team, for low to medium risk searches the tactical officers can recruit four or five uniformed members and work together.

When striving for consistency within an organization, we're able to act as force multipliers and enhance our overall efficacy. Imagine how valuable it would be to have tactical operators and uniformed officers arriving on scene at a mass murder in progress and be able to operate cohesively.

If you dare to dream, you can strive for consistency across different agencies. Logistical issues such as a poor or complete lack of communication between different agencies or operating inconsistencies has contributed to the failure of many major operations. The massive hostage taking at the school in Beslan, Russia, in 2004 is a prime example of this. Special forces groups were on the ground in a holding patterns for days before they were able organize themselves, while children inside were being absolutely brutalized, mostly due to lack of coordination and communication among different agencies. For an essential and disturbing read, pick up *Terror at Beslan: A Russian Tragedy with Lessons for America's Schools*, by John Giduck, to learn from this tragedy.

Closer to home, many incidents, especially mass murders, have two or three different agencies responding simultaneously. If our communication is consistent and we streamline predictable logistical issues, such as having an emergency use of a common radio talk group, we make it that much harder for the bad guys to win.

Training for Reality

In addition to consistency and simplicity, we need to accept some realities. Policing is a complex profession and tactics are only a small part of it. There are many attributes that will determine a person's success in the field of policing, so we need to embrace the fact that every member of our services has strengths and weaknesses that are unique to them. Not all the people we train are going to have a high tactical IQ, but as trainers, we need to recognize that they will have other strengths. It's our job to maximize the strengths of our students and minimize their weaknesses, but more importantly, to teach a simple system that can be mastered by everyone. Being honest about who we need to train is crucial. This is not only a police training issue, this is a human issue, as you will recall from the principle of **individual differences**, discussed in chapter 4.

Decreasing Skills Erosion

Just as important is recognizing the limited amount of time to train and the reality that these skills will perish if not used. It is because of this reality that our training needs to be as simple as possible but also provides students with the skills and tools to continue to *self-learn.* Continued learning after the training event can be accomplished by conducting critical incident debriefing after field experiences. By debriefing in the field or in the briefing room after the fact, we replay and reconstruct the incident. When we act in the manner in which we've been trained and refer to that training to honestly evaluate our own and others' performance as a group, we can decrease the amount of skills erosion exponentially. If we debrief incidents in this manner, every event becomes a training event. Remember the principle of **use and disuse**? Use it or lose it. Distributing or making available online some training lesson plans to students will them assist in reviewing training material, and debriefing field performances will solidify long-term retention.

We need to be honest about what we expect our officers to do. Are they really going to be able to access and perform two, three, or four different formations under stress based on the limited amount of time we have for training? Probably not. What is worse is that the time spent learning new formations robs us of the valuable repetitions required to internalize a basic skill set. It's not only ineffective, it's counterproductive! If we train properly, especially by using the instructional discussions I've introduced, we can ingrain the principles so that instead of giving our students the answers, they will be equipped to come up with the answers themselves.

By embracing simplicity, by acknowledging the truths of who we are training, and by being realistic about what we are training them for, we can achieve a simple, single, flexible formation that officers can access in the field: one that will equip them with the best tactics for the highest-probability situations.

The result of this training is a moving organism made up of principle-based and tactically sound members, capable of morphing and adapting to their ever-changing mission and environment.

Kind of like an amoeba.

Acknowledgments and Sources

Unless otherwise noted, all illustrations drawn by Sandra C. Barnes (sandrabarnes.design).

Chapter 1

Chapter epigraph from Lao Tzu, *Tao Te Ching* (Oxford Press, 1891; Dover Publications, 1997), chap. 76.

Chapter 2

Sun Tzu, *The Art of War* (Shamhbala Publications, 1998).

OODA Loop Graphic is from www.usconcealedcarry.com/blog/situational-awareness-using-o-o-d-loop/.

John R. Boyd, "Destruction and Creation" (U.S. Army Command and General Staff College, 3 September 1976), www.goalsys.com/books/documents/DESTRUCTION_AND_CREATION.pdf.

For more on the OODA Loop, see Brett and Kate McKay, "The Tao of Boyd: How to Master the OODA Loop" (29 October 2018), at https://www.artofmanliness.com/articles/ooda-loop/.

Charles Remsberg, *Street Survival* series (Calibre Press, 1980).

Research of the Force Science Institute can be seen at at www.forcescience.org.

Chapter 3

Chapter epigraph from Sun Tzu, *Art of War* (Shamhbala Publications, 1998), chap. 3.

Chapter 4

Chapter epigraph from Bruce Lee, *Tao of Jeet Kune Do* (Black Belt Books, 1975), p. 11.

Bruce K. Siddle, *Sharpening the Warrior's Edge: The Psychology and Science of Training* (PPCT Management Systems, 1995) Survival Stress Definition.

Bruce K. Siddle, *PPCT Defensive Tactics Instructor Manual* (Pressure Point Control Tactics Research Publications, February 2005). The summary of motor skills is taken from chap. 1, p. 4; the descriptions of different types of perceptual narrowing is from chap. 1, pp. 3–4.

Dave Grossman and Loren W. Christensen, *On Combat: The Psychology and Physiology of Deadly Conflict in War and Peace* (PPCT Research Publications, 2004).

Thomas Baechle and Roger Earle, *Essentials of Strength Training and Conditioning* (National Strength and Conditioning Association, 1994). Summary of the Six General Principles of Training is from p. 46ff.

John J. Ratey M.D., A User's Guide to the Brain: *Perception, Attention, and the Four Theaters of the Brain.* (Vantage Books, 2001)

Chapter 5

Chapter epigraph from Dave Grossman and Loren W. Christensen, *On Combat: The Psychology and Physiology of Deadly Conflict in War and Peace* (PPCT Research Publications, 2004).

Grossman's anecdote about his grandson is from a live talk he presented at Bulletproof Mind in Grand Forks, ND, 2012.

Chapter 6

Chapter epigraph by Xun Kuang from Liu Xiang, *Xunzi,* Book 8 (*Ruxiao,* "The Teachings of the Ru"), chap. 11.

Chapter 7

Ron Borsch's research into rapid mass murders is published in regularly on his **PACT** Consultant Group's Training **Newsletter.** A free newsletter is available to those who request one at rbi0075@juno.com

My sincerest thanks to Mr. Borsch for his permission to cite his research.

Pie chart drawn by the author

Chapter 8

John Giduck, Terror at Beslan: A Russian Tragedy with Lessons for America's Schools (Archangel Publishing Group, 2005).

Special Thanks...

- *Randy Lahaie of toughenup.com for his mentorship, friendship, guidance and encouragement throughout my career and whose help made this project believable and possible*

- *Sandra Barnes of sandrabarnes.design for her original artwork and unending patience with a subject matter she knew nothing about but had the professionalism to learn*

- *Maureen Epp for her patience in the editing of this text.*

- *Ron Borsch at rbi0075@juno.com who graciously allowed me to use his life saving research to support the key argument of this book. His research is groundbreaking and when many people covet their findings, he shares them selflessly for the greater good*